POKE THE BEAR WITHIN!

PROPEL YOURSELF TO GROWTH AND SUCCESS

AF703709

Srinivas Krishnan

notionpress.com

INDIA • SINGAPORE • MALAYSIA

Copyright © Srinivas Krishnan 2023
All Rights Reserved.

ISBN

Hardcase 979-8-89133-365-9
Paperback 979-8-89133-363-5

This book has been published with all efforts taken to make the material error-free after the consent of the author. However, the author and the publisher do not assume and hereby disclaim any liability to any party for any loss, damage, or disruption caused by errors or omissions, whether such errors or omissions result from negligence, accident, or any other cause.

While every effort has been made to avoid any mistake or omission, this publication is being sold on the condition and understanding that neither the author nor the publishers or printers would be liable in any manner to any person by reason of any mistake or omission in this publication or for any action taken or omitted to be taken or advice rendered or accepted on the basis of this work. For any defect in printing or binding the publishers will be liable only to replace the defective copy by another copy of this work then available.

I dedicate this book to my better half, Jayashree, our two lovely children, Krishnan and Lakshita, my late parents, my siblings, and my friends from school and college.

This collection of anecdotes would not have been possible but for the memorable time we spent in Jakarta as a family, in the company of some lovely Indians expats who became friends for life.

Contents

Concepts with QR Code Links

Acknowledgements

Several influences encouraged me to pen my thoughts, from my childhood, adolescence, teenage, and adult life.

My paternal grandma and maternal grandpa's deep-rooted affection.

My parents' wish to see me and my three siblings successful, which made me push myself harder in almost all walks of life.

The boost I received from my school friends, my childhood neighbours, my friends in Chennai and Hong Kong, my spiritual masters in Hong Kong, Jakarta and India, my acquaintances in Jakarta and my colleagues at Crown Worldwide Group in Indonesia and India.

The encouragement from many friends to express my thoughts on how I waded through challenges and capitalised on opportunities in different countries.

I thank all of them.

I also thank the power of the divine for giving me an opportunity to bring out the best version of myself in different challenging situations, at times alone and at other times, with the support of family and colleagues.

Foreword

Link: https://youtu.be/gnUzvJbt-qA

For the past 58 years, I've had the opportunity to manage many people as my company, Crown Worldwide Group, has grown from a tiny three-man office to a global entity with thousands of staff members. Over these years, I've become a keen observer of what differentiates members of our team, particularly how some staff excel and rise to higher levels in the company.

Management, after all, is the ability of a person to willingly take on a leadership role — whether it be of a small team or a much larger one — and determine how he or she can get the most dynamic performance from those who report to them to achieve or exceed the company's goals. This can be tricky because people are all different and, as such, they are motivated differently. However, some leaders have a keen sense of all those in their team and can determine the best approach to have them excel individually as well as for the team. Indeed, only a few people have this skill.

Some leaders tend to be brusque, such as you might find in the military, while some are more caring and have a natural concern for the welfare of the people they are leading. Both styles can be effective in getting results and achieving the goal if they can get their team to understand the objective and work together to achieve it.

Srinivas Krishnan has been an interesting study in this regard. He's a soft-spoken man, but can be firm when he has to. The key feature of his personality is that he is determined. He knows what his goal is and manages, with a degree of flexibility, to allow his large team to strive for success.

Now, after years of successful management, he has told the story of what he has learned and applied, and the resultant success he has achieved during his career. It's the wonderful story of the success of a man who entered the business world with no experience but great determination. The story of the early days of his career, managing people of a different nationality in Indonesia, in a company that was underperforming when he arrived. The story of how he became a vital part of that company and a trusted advisor to the general manager.

This is the story of a man who would set realistic goals for himself and, when he reached each goal, set a *higher* goal. His success is obvious (and he now manages a large region that continually excels for our company), yet he is still setting higher goals. Through it all, his deep love of his family and of the sport of cricket has allowed him to have a well-rounded life, blending personal success with personal happiness.

There is much to be learned from the messages in this book. I'm sure this book will serve as an inspiration to those who read it.

– James Thompson
Chairman and Founder, Crown Worldwide Group

Link: https://youtube.com/watch?v=wZfFw5Gmlw4&feature=shared

What I love about the book is the contents come straight from the heart – the heart of a guy who started from a very humble background and worked his way up – with determination, rigid in adhering to certain principles and core values, and yet, beautifully adapting to new situations and ever-evolving to stay relevant and succeed. Am proud of what he has achieved in his life and career so far. I've known him for 35 years now since the time we were colleagues in Boehringer Mannheim in Mumbai. We have continued to stay in touch as he moved to Hong Kong, then Jakarta, Indonesia, and back to Mumbai.

Coming to the book, contains several helpful lessons distilled from both Srini's struggles as well as his wins interspersed with several interesting anecdotes from his life over the years.

There are helpful QR code links to short YouTube videos embodying the various lessons. That linkage is an interesting innovation and should certainly appeal to today's youngsters.

If I had to pick my favourite part of the book, that is chapter 4 which starts with the sentence "If knowledge is power, then learning is a super-power". And then Srini goes on to illustrate multiple ways of learning. And I know for a fact that Srini is a fan of continuous learning and unlearning – 2 key examples are him doing a mid-career MBA from Chicago School of Business, picking up long-distance running in 2015, and then running a full marathon 5 years later.

Srini, more power to this honest endeavor of yours to selflessly share various life-lessons in an easy and flowing manner.

Wish you, the book, and its reader's lots of fulfilment.

– **Raju Venkatraman**
Leadership Coach and Career Advisor,
Former CFO and Head of Strategy,
Walt Disney Company – South East Asia

Link: https://www.youtube.com/watch?v=8os38J0SRcA

– **K. Jayshankar**
Life and Leadership Coach
Managing Director, Empowered Learning Systems

Link: https://youtube.com/watch?v=Z6yN6dkYoBs&feature=shared

I just finished reading Srini's new book 'Poke the Bear Within!' a fabulous book, and a very easy read. I couldn't keep it down. Srini has captured very well the life lessons that he has learned in this book. In fact, I love the structure he has used. His own sort of challenge that he has faced in his life and then how he dealt with it and then there are key takeaways from each chapter. It's a fabulous book with a lot of learnings. It's a book that is very rich and I certainly benefitted from reading that book. So, I would recommend it to anybody who would like to read it and learn from it. Thank

– Rajesh Ganesh
Leader, Board Member, CEO
Alumni

Link: https://www.youtube.com/watch?v=BB0NhygIP68

– Milind Kamath
Vice President, Technology, Accenture

Link: https://www.youtube.com/watch?v=oUBWVKg6SDY

Hi Srinivas, many congratulations on completing your first book 'Poke The Bear Within!'. It's packed with life lessons. One of the attributes I have seen in Srinivas consistently over so many years is his determination. I am Ramamoorthy Rajagopal his childhood friend and one of the Lucky Seven he has referred to in Chapter Two. It's indeed a proud moment for all of us that I've been watching Srinivas achieve one milestone after the other. It's not very easy to achieve excellence in varied fields of academics, profession, sports, music, literature and spirituality. In addition, personal, family, and social obligations cannot be attributed to luck for coincidence. It's all a result of a certain approach to life, a set of values, principles, and framework that Srinivas has diligently been implementing and practicing over so many years and that's precisely what you will find in his book. I'm sure the new generation will find this book immensely useful, there are so many valuable lessons to be learned, which will help all of us achieve excellence and happiness both professionally and personally. As we speak Srinivas, I am sure you've already set your eyes on the next goal and beginning to sketch it. I wish you continued success and all the very best for the book launch. Thank you.

– R Ramamoorthy
Chief Operating Officer, DSP MERRYL LYNCH

* * * * *

Preface

Executive Leadership Team (ELT) member advising the Board of Directors of Crown Worldwide Group; Regional Managing Director – South Asia, Crown Worldwide Group; ex-Finance Director – Indonesia, Crown Worldwide Group; ex-professional international cricketer; international speaker; holder of multiple degrees; marathon runner; philanthropist; husband; father.

People know me by all these labels today.

But was I like this from day one? No. Was I born with a silver spoon No. Did I know right in the beginning that I would end up being all this one day? No, not at all!

And yet, here I am, leading a deeply fulfilling, happy life. I am rich. I don't mean it in the narrow monetary sense, though life has blessed me with enough money too. I am rich in every sense of the word: spiritually, emotionally, in terms of relationships, experiences and memories, in terms of the impact of my work, values and life lessons, in terms of hope and happiness. And of course, in terms of gratitude — for what life has given me and continues to give me every day.

But for all these gains, there was a time when life was a struggle. A quagmire of confusion, uncertainty and anxiety.

Making the most of an uncertain life

Link 1: https://youtu.be/
X5FymyNSUEQ?si=0yRxRclrFWA57PbY

> Making the Most of Uncertain Life: As some of you may be aware, yesterday's hot but shocking news about the sad demise of the Marketing person from Tata Motors who was in charge of the Electric Vehicle. He was keeping fit, and his medical reports gave good remarks, which were taken a few months back and he suddenly passed away. This indicates that for a number of us, life is going to be uncertain and short. So what do we make out of it? Let us kill our silly egos, let us forgive people who hurt us, let us truly love, let us learn to burn our temper, let us laugh loudly, and let us not avoid any opportunity that allows us to make smile.

If I, an average person from a lower-middle-class family from a suburb of the city of Bombay (as Mumbai was called when I was born; I refer to the city by this name throughout this book), have achieved whatever I have, it is by dint of certain lessons, principles and values I picked up along the way from various situations and people. I have found that there is no school better than life, and I have tried to learn as much as possible from this finest of schools.

I know that by following the same lessons, principles and values, you too can reach great heights, make a mark in your chosen fields, and lead a happy, successful life. Which is why I have written this book. Though there are factors such as luck and destiny, to a large extent, it is possible for us to shape our lives through our thoughts, habits, decisions, discipline and commitment and by leveraging the prevailing ecosystem. I have peppered my narration with incidents, situations, and decisions from my life so that you can understand my message better. You will find me referring to a few parts of my life more than once on these pages. This is because I have written the chapters thematically, and in certain places, it is important to refer to these parts from the angle of that chapter.

I hope you like this book and find it useful. If it helps you improve your life by even a few notches, I will be happy. As you read it, you may find it useful to underline certain parts or take notes on the aspects that resonate strongly with you. And you may like to return to certain chapters for a closer reading later on.

The power of this book lies not just in its message but also in the reader embracing the message and living it day after day. I sincerely hope you will practise whatever resonates with you. Feel free to connect what you think of the book and share your opinions on life in general, or on a specific situation you are facing. If you are an anxious, busy parent with children in their early 20s and are looking for tangible ideas to help them plan their future, you may get fresh insights from this book. You can get in touch with me through my website, www.srinivassk.com, and my email id, pokethebearwithin@gmail.com. I am available for chats on weekends.

Happy reading! And happy living!

– Srinivas Krishnan
Regional Managing Director – South Asia,
Crown Worldwide Group

Chapter 1

The Sky is the Limit

We play different roles in every stage of life. And each role comes with expectations attached, some more important than others. As children, we are expected to do well in academics and extra-curricular activities. When we enter college, we are expected to get good jobs in the next few years. As working professionals, we have to contend with the continuous expectation of our clients, bosses or both, that we will deliver on our KRAs. Other than this, we are expected to be 'good' friends, children, siblings, colleagues, etc.

Against this backdrop, I have learned something invaluable: always expect more from yourself than from others.

Having expectations from others can hurt you, especially when they fall short of your expected level and don't deliver the goods. On the other hand, expecting something from yourself can only inspire you — a lot. If you want to improve the luminosity of inspiration — that is, if you want to get more out of the bouts of inspiration — you have to keep enriching your capabilities and skills methodically.

I have been part of a team on several occasions — at work, in academic projects, in sports, and on the spiritual front. Terms would be dictated and rules laid down by the leaders for others to comply with. There would be stiff targets and tough goals. From my experiences in such teams, I have realised that often I do my bit to complete the tasks as per the demands. And I expect my teammates to do their part. Sometimes, I may even extend a hand to help them complete their bit. And then, I hope that, together, we will achieve our collective goal.

Expectation vs acceptance

Link 1: https://youtu.be/q7bUSZNHt3M
Duration: 01:28 Mts.

> Expectation versus acceptance: A number of us are involved in serving the society, some close associates, some acquaintances and what we are looking forward to is the happiness chemical called the peace of mind. In the course of our service, we note that things don't go as we want. This is where we run into problems. Expectations of things in the way we want at times, can actually lead us to tears, whereas acceptance can bring us cheers. Acceptance of life as things are, should be accepted as the normal course of natural outcome. Unrealistic expectations will lead to disappointment and will lead to the loss of the beautiful gift, which is essentially the peace of mind, for which we have set out on our course to serve society. Easier said than done, but worth an attempt.

However, I have found this thinking to be foolhardy. Why? Because we are most likely not aware of the situations our team members are in — physically, emotionally or psychologically. This may sound obvious to some and stupid to some others. But quite often, we do ignore this aspect of life — that is to look at things from another person's point of view. For example, it is imperative that those who play cricket professionally have to maintain peak fitness — physically and mentally. This is a pre-condition for an above-average performance. But this does not always happen; just because you and I are prepared, it does not mean that others will be similarly prepared to take on the challenge.

The onus then falls on us to set an example, in the hope that others will be prompted to follow suit. Whether they do so or not is their choice, but take the lead we must. A continuous focus on incremental improvement, with ruthless discipline and boring consistency, will likely enrich us. It will also prompt many others to catch our vibes and hop on board the same approach. Of course, a few others are likely to be left behind by convention; it is best to leave them with their choice.

Just think. If each of us starts with a score of 100 today, *a mere 1% daily improvement* can lead us to a score of 3,780 at the end of the year. However, if we allow the status quo to remain, we will find ourselves sliding back at the rate of 1% a day. And, by the end of a year, we would have slid down to a score of a mere 26. If we allow this to happen when we are part of a team, we can imagine the fate of the team.

Learning new things regularly

Link 2: https://youtu.be/l8yrHVA48nM
Duration: 00:41 Mts.

One of the signs of progress in life is to find out what is new that we have learned. In today's order of disruption, we need to continuously keep learning and educate ourselves because as Robin Sharma says, learning and education are inoculation against disruption, otherwise, life gets boring to be within the limits of what you know.

On enriching oneself

Link 3: https://youtu.be/3hOPd5rVMFY
Duration: 00:45 Mts.

> The relationship between enrichment and inspiration: Always expect more from yourself than from others; because expectation from others can hurt you when you fall short of your level whereas expectation from yourself can inspire you a lot. If you want to improve the luminosity of inspiration you need to continuously keep enriching yourself with skills, capabilities, and competencies methodically.

But this seems easier said than done, given the hectic pace and vagaries of life. So, to enable this, one has to develop the habit of taking a few steps back from the action and introspecting calmly, pausing one's frenetic thoughts. The habit of calming the mind is immensely beneficial. When we develop this habit, some people around us, in our ecosystem, may call us crazy. Because they may be taking life easy and taking things as they come. Their minds are beehives of humdrum thoughts. But if we were to merely follow them, how different will we be from them? How will we carve out the path *we* want in life, achieve the things *we* want, utilise the talents and flair *we* have been gifted with?

Which is why, if you want to improve the luminosity of inspiration, you must keep enriching yourself methodically.

Spend time alone. Most of the obstacles to success and happiness come from undervaluing ourselves and overvaluing others. This is because we don't look at ourselves in the mirror often, other than while brushing our teeth or combing our hair. We have to spend time alone to count our blessings and introspect. This also helps us understand what makes us happy — what we *should be* pursuing. Definitely, this is not casy. But it is easier than you think. Try doing it.

Why you should spend time alone

Link 4: https://youtu.be/iu2vRjxtlfg
Duration: 00:42 Mts.

> The benefits of spending time alone: Most of the obstacles to happiness come from us undervaluing ourselves and overvaluing others. This happens because we don't tend to look at ourselves in the mirror, more often except for brushing our teeth or combing our hair. One ought to spend time alone to count one's blessings. Identify what makes us happy and pursue that which gives us happiness. This is a hard but true fact of life, try doing it.

I have learned that there are two indicators of greatness: success and happiness. The success of a person is measured not by their wealth, education, or beauty but the loyalty of their heart and the humility of their soul. How do we develop these two qualities? Loyalty comes from absolute passion and engagement. Humility comes from not getting carried away by what we achieve but by intensely searching for the next big thing in whatever we are involved in. As leadership guru Robin Sharma says, 'World class is a dangerous sport. Excellence is a continuous journey.'

I have found, not just from having practised it myself but also from the lives of several others, that if we inculcate these traits in ourselves, there is a very good chance that greatness will come to us.

Success v/s happiness

Link 5: https://youtu.be/QFY9rfC4ZHs
Duration: 00:49 Mts.

> Chasing success versus happiness: Life is not a music player where you can always choose to run the song you want, in the name of scoring success. In fact, it is akin to a radio where you have to adjust yourself to every frequency to use and learn to enjoy it. Remember this is what gives happiness. While success is manufactured in the mind, happiness is developed in the soul. Are you ready to tune into your soulfulness?

Clarity of thought is essential to solve many problems. Which is why the 'S-square of solutions' matters in life: Silence and Smiling Lips. We come across many problems. To solve these, we must be clear in our thinking. Train your mind to be silent from time to time. Because silence brings with it calm, composure and clarity of thought. Another trait that helps enormously in solving problems and overcoming difficulties is a cheerful, positive disposition. The power of a smile, though known, is still severely underrated. Speaking lips can hardly solve any problem in life, while closed lips can solve *some* problems. But smiling lips can solve many problems forever. So learn to keep smiling and be silent; you will find yourself solving all your problems with this deadly combination.

The S-square of solutions for life

Link 6: https://youtu.be/wFafo-9hR6E
Duration: 00:59 Mts.

> We will talk about the Esquire of solutions of life. We come across many problems, and it requires clarity of thought to solve these. Train yourself to get your mind to remain silent, because silence leads to a high possibility of clarity of thoughts. Speaking lips can hardly solve any issues in life, closed lips can solve some issues, whereas smiling lips can solve many problems forever. So, learn to remain silent and, at the same time keep smiling and enjoy the deadly combination to solve all your problems.

Another credo I swear by is 'easy and crazy'. Anything is easy when we are crazy about it, and nothing is easy when we are lazy about it. The only way to become crazy about something is to do one thing at a time, really well. What we need for this is focus. If you look at amazing world-changers, they have a masterful way of focussing on one thing at a time and saying no to everything else. That *one* important project, that *one thing* you are creating, that *one thing* you want to see through to the end: focus on this to make things easy for you. This way, you will also create something of lasting significance and value. Something you can be justifiably proud about.

On making things easy like crazy

Link 7: https://youtu.be/G2PfQEe7uFI
Duration: 00:54 Mts.

> Easy and crazy: Everything is easy, when we are crazy about it and nothing is easy when we are lazy about it. The only way to become crazy is to do one thing at a time really well. What we need for this purpose is focus and if you look at amazing world changers, they have a masterful way of thoughtfully saying "NO" to other things, when we are focusing on one thing at a time. So, focus on "One thing" to make things easy for you like crazy.

Living like this, with all the qualities I described just now, will endow us with happiness, success and a rich life overall. And it may well prompt a few others around us to do the same, thereby lifting the spirit of the entire team or ecosystem. And this, in turn, may help us achieve the larger goals of life in any context — business, sports, spirituality or in any other realm.

In my college days, even as I was working my way towards a professional career, the unfulfilled passion of playing serious cricket was lurking in a corner of my mind. This was in Bombay, where the game has always been competitive. A few years later, after a few twists and turns in life, I took up a job in Jakarta, Indonesia. There, I was part of a cricket team named Senayan. I had the honour of playing with several others from different parts of South Asia and South East Asia, such as India, Sri Lanka, Indonesia, Singapore and Pakistan. I have had the privilege of playing with people from the UK, Australia, New Zealand, Fiji and South Africa as well, and understanding their cultures. There came a point in time when weekend matches became important and serious. So much so that the outcome of a weekend match decided the players' mood for the following week.

If we were to even *dream* of winning the trophy, which was the outcome of a series of matches played over the season (September to May 2000), we had to get our act together immediately and lift the side in various aspects such as fitness, skill, focus, the hunger to win and on-field performance. The then Country Head of Crown Indonesia, the late Mr. Rick McCarty, was kind enough to authorise membership for me to the famous recreation club ISCI (International Sports Club of Indonesia) in Jakarta. Those days, I was working with Crown Worldwide Group in Jakarta as the Financial Controller for their troubled operations in Indonesia. (I am with Crown even now, but in a different role and place. More about this later).

The key to the door of personal excellence

Link 8: https://youtu.be/CieNuZaZKMc
Duration: 01:06 Mts.

The keys to the door of personal excellence: Excellence is defined as something that can be achieved by people because they have that inner belief that is better than the surrounding circumstances that prevail. What are those things and their beliefs? First of all the will to win, second desire to succeed and third thing is the urge to give the full potential at all costs. These are keys which helps one to unlock the door of personal excellence. With these things in mind, you go ahead with confidence for approaching anything, you will succeed, and these are not inborn or genetic. Try it out.

The Sky is the Limit

This was a great opportunity for me to realise my dream and my expectation of myself on the cricket field. I knew I had the option of indulging in a few beers at the club's bar every evening. Or, I could attempt to learn other things like squash, swimming, golf and rowing. But I chose to set a gruelling routine by practising my game of cricket on the lush green field that was being maintained so well by the groundskeepers. I decided that this was a God-given opportunity to pursue my dream of improving my game and playing professional cricket at the highest level. And I grabbed this opportunity with both hands!

While a Saturday session at the nets was a ritual, I would go to ISCI almost every evening after work, wading through the heavy South Jakarta traffic for an hour and a half, merely for a one-hour practice session. Those days we didn't have much entertainment, other than socialising with friends or with the Indian diaspora to build our network, or watch soap operas on TV with the family. So this almost-daily ritual of playing cricket let me focus on improving my game. Eventually, I was able to do my bit to help the Senayan team win the Jakarta Cricket League and several other trophies. I was elected to lead the team in just a few seasons! The added responsibility of leading the team to victory meant that I needed a winning combination of players. My players could be of any nationality, but they had to be the best. All that mattered was that they have the talent, dedication and drive to win.

Eventually, Crown Worldwide Group started sponsoring the Senayan team in Jakarta Cricket League, leading to some level of visibility for the brand. A series of successes in local tournaments led me to apply for a slot in the Java provincial team. I got selected for this team purely based on my past performances. And finally, I even represented Indonesia in the ICC World Cup qualifiers in 2005 and 2007! This was really big for me.

To play for the national team is undoubtedly a dream for any professional player, irrespective of their background. The selection criteria for the Indonesia national team were quite stringent. Also, as in other spheres of life, one had to contend with politics there too. But eventually, my performance paved the way for me to represent the country. I used to take things quite seriously in life, and I was quite serious about playing for Indonesia. Playing for the national team amidst competing commitments and complex choices in life, without sacrificing my work and while devoting adequate time to my family, tested the limits of my will power and my dedication to the game.

All this was possible only due to ruthless discipline (regular exercise during the week, adequate rest in the form of proper sleep and daily practice on the ground). My point is, each of us faces a multitude of options. We should choose what gives us happiness and success in *one* important aspect of life. I know from experience that this will almost always lead us to happiness and success in other aspects of life too.

For instance, during those years in Jakarta, even as I started doing well on the cricket field, I began to perform well at my job also, solving one longstanding problem after another. This prompted my company to send me on complex assignments to other countries such as Italy, South Africa, Hong Kong, Malaysia, Russia, Philippines, Vietnam, Singapore and China. This went on from the years 2000 to 2009.

You can call these achievements a stroke of luck. But I define luck as 'a combination of choices created, opportunities explored and chances taken at the right moments'. In other words, by constantly honing our skills and level of preparation, and focussing on what we want, we are more likely to attract lucrative and interesting opportunities. And this is what the world calls luck!

What makes the present generation of youngsters more privileged than the earlier ones is the low-cost access to an almost-unlimited amount of information and many more career options to choose from. Instead of grabbing what is handy and taking things easy, one should therefore plan their time, be calm enough to think through the abundant options, be mature enough to decide the right set of circumstances appropriate to their situation, develop their capabilities and shamelessly seek help from parents and experts. All this will help them decide what is right for them and build happy careers for themselves.

Through this book, I am sharing the precious lessons I have learnt in life. These have helped me grow tremendously as a person and professional and have given me a fulfilling, happy and thriving life. All of us are a work-in-progress. But looking back at where I started from, I realise I have come a long, long way and tasted success in no small measure. And I have done it by always focussing on pushing the bar higher and higher up i.e., raising my level in every aspect of life, day after day after day. And the journey continues, with the gift of a smile, admiration for many and envy for a few.

Key takeaways

Capacity = self-awareness + actions + choices (Source: The book *No Limits* by John Maxwell)

Never act unless your mind is guided by calm and happy thoughts. Even your worst enemy cannot harm you as much as your own negative thoughts.

Making the right choice entails a long pause, deep thought and taking advantage of the prevailing ecosystem.

Expect more from yourself than from others. Keep raising the bar for yourself in whatever you do.

The rub-off effect of expecting more from yourself can improve the ability and performance of your entire team or ecosystem.

Please provide your views, comments, feedback and share what parts of this chapter resonates with you here

Link: https://srinivas.powervisionelectrical.co.in/chapter-1-the-sky-is-the-limit/

Chapter 2

Simple Lessons, Big Inspiration

You are strong when you know your weakness.
You are self-aware when you realise your flaws.
You are wise when you learn from your mistakes.

I come from humble beginnings. But if I have still come a long way, it is, to a large extent, due to the huge doses of inspiration and the various little lessons I have received from certain friends, colleagues and members of my family. While the lessons helped me choose the right path and make the right decisions, the inspiration has propped me up during my low phases and kept my morale high. My story is a great example of how familial circumstances and people close to us can shape our lives and careers.

In the pre-Independence era, my paternal grandpa and grandma eked out their livelihood in a small place called Lakshmangudi in Thanjavur district of Tamil Nadu in India. My grandpa was a cook at a humble eatery. He barely earned enough to provide two square meals a day to his family of 7—himself, Grandma, and their five children. Diabetes took away Grandpa at the rather young age of 52. Those days, there was no cure for diabetes; it was often a terminal disease. After his passing, it was the owner of the eatery where Grandpa had been the cook who took care of the family. So you can imagine the difficult times they lived through.

My dad was born in a small town called Thripunithura in the state of Kerala. After finishing his matriculation, he had no choice but to come to a city like Bombay to find a job, borrowing clothes from his elderly neighbours! He had to find a way to fend for himself. Initially, he made a humble living working in sweatshops. And then, he got an opportunity to interview with Life Insurance Corporation of India, (hereafter termed as LIC elsewhere in this book) one of India's leading insurance companies. He got a job as an assistant, in spite of speaking only broken English. Keen to upskill himself, he then learnt shorthand and typing from an institute. Burning the candle on many nights and working even over the weekends, Dad steadily established himself in LIC and began rising up the ranks there.

As this was happening, he brought his four siblings and his mother from their village to Bombay, one by one. He helped them settle down in the big city. He got married. I am the third of my parents' four children. Dad showed us that working hard is the way to come up in life. And he indicated the struggle you have to go through if you don't study well and get the right academic qualifications. My keenness to acquire solid academic qualifications and keep upskilling myself through advanced education came from my father.

I also learned from my father how to be a self-made, considerate, systematic and frugal person. He has been a huge inspiration and guiding force for me.

During my childhood, I was my grandma's favourite. Through her influence, I used to get almost whatever I wanted. Until the age of 11, I was only an average student. I never cared about serious things like career. Come to think of it, I didn't take most things seriously. It was around the age of 11 that I started realising that I would have to study hard to come up in life — thanks partly to my grandma and partly to my dad. Grandma used to motivate me and persuade me to focus on my studies despite all the constraints of a joint family, the chief of which was that we would have frequent visitors over the weekends and evenings.

At around the same time, my father gave me a rude shock by shifting me from a Malayalam-medium section (in which I had thus far learned Maths, History, Geography and Science) to a Marathi-medium section in the same school. He thought this (being a matriculate with an ability to speak Marathi, the local language) would equip me better to get at least a basic graduate degree, so I could find a job in LIC, the company where he worked. I could be offered a job in Bombay as his lineal descendant. He never thought I was serious enough to build a great career for myself.

But for me, this was a drastic change. My new class had about 20 students from different parts of India. I was someone who had learned Hindi and Malayalam before learning English, so I faced a steep learning curve in this new school. This was how, at the tender age of 11, I entered the world of sea changes in life.

Though my grandma had studied only until 3rd grade in school, she had gathered a lot of wisdom from the school of life. And tales from Hindu mythology had taught her what is right and what is wrong. She passed this wisdom on to me. She used to tell me that the key to being happy is knowing that you have the power to choose what to accept, what to side-step and what to let go. She also used to tell me that if we work on something a little bit every day, we will end up with something massive over a period of time. Isn't this what all the management gurus of today say — that several incremental improvements over a period of time lead to gigantic results? I have applied Grandma's principles in every facet of my life, especially my career. And this has stood me in good stead.

Instead of focussing on the outcome, I've focussed on the process, the people and the circumstances around me. Instead of cutting corners, I have always tried to ensure that I stand my ground even in the face of stiff opposition. Grandma used to tell me that instead of worrying about what we cannot control, we must shift our energy to what we *can* control. And to what we can *create*.

This is exactly what I did when I was in Indonesia. I noticed a massive devaluation of the Indonesian currency in 1997 (related to the Asian financial crisis). Most of my colleagues in Sales were forcing me to continue invoicing our company's customers in Rupiah, the local currency, even though it was nose-diving. But I took a stand that we had to protect our company's interests and so, should charge customers in dollars. And this helped us turn the fortunes of the company around in Indonesia in a short period of time!

Another valuable lesson Grandma imparted to me is that relationships are not built by forcing others to understand us. They are built by giving them the confidence that *we* will be careful enough to understand them. This nugget helped me stay the course and win the confidence of my team in Jakarta, when I joined Crown Worldwide there in 1997. Most of my colleagues were Indonesians. The culture of the place was different from that of Hong Kong or India, the two countries I had lived in before. The language was different too. But the body language and the calmness with which I used to treat my colleagues and others helped me settle down in that place and build a career over the next 13 years. I was forewarned; my predecessor, an expat from one of the countries in Asia-Pacific, had been sent back for his arrogant attitude towards the Indonesian staff.

Grandma would also say that if taking a particular step in life makes you happy, and if you've given it enough thought, go ahead and take that step even if it doesn't make sense to others. This belief has helped me take a number of major decisions. For instance, deciding to shift from Mulund College of Commerce in the suburbs of Bombay to RA Podar College of Commerce & Economics, located in South Bombay. I had to leave my old collegemates and the familiar setup of Mulund College. This brought about a significant change in my outlook towards life, especially in understanding how wealthy people (of whom there were far more in Podar than in Mulund College) moved and behaved. It also helped me become a better cricketer, thanks to better coaching and infrastructure at Podar.

Similarly, when I wanted to pursue my career outside India, I decided to go to the Far East (Hong Kong) when most other Indians were looking to go to the Middle East. With some patience and luck, I got a job in Hong Kong, though I had to give my employer a commitment that I'd work with him for at least 3 years. This, in a 100% employment economy, where it was very easy to quit one company and get a job in another company on the same day. I maintained my 3-year commitment to this company. And when this period was coming to an end in 1994, I decided to move out of Hong Kong and go to Jakarta, a much less developed place than Hong Kong in the conventional sense! I got an offer from Crown Worldwide Group to join their Jakarta office in Indonesia, and I accepted it.

While my colleagues, friends and acquaintances thought this to be akin to going from Toronto to Timbuktu, I was quite happy. I knew I was taking an important step in my life. And I proved myself right when I had a vibrant stint in Crown in Jakarta for 13 years, delivering results for the company and scaling the performance. My family and I enjoyed a vibrant social and personal life too.

My contrarian approach was evident yet again, when, after 13 happy years in Jakarta, my wife and I decided to move back to Bombay with our children. Many of my colleagues and others were shocked as to why we were leaving the comfortable expat life of Jakarta, and its tax-free perks, and returning to overcrowded, space-starved, polluted Bombay. But my wife and I knew that our aging parents needed our support and that we had to be by their side. And so, off we came to Bombay, where we have lived ever since.

So you see, I have taken a number of important decisions in my career and personal life based on the invaluable teachings of my grandma. A couple of her other nuggets of wisdom that have helped me enormously are:

- In any situation, do not assume anything. Instead, ask the person(s) concerned, so you get the right information from the horse's mouth. Get your doubts clarified by them, not by someone else.
- If we stop expecting anything from others, we will automatically remove their power to hurt our feelings. Hurt and sorrow arise from our sense of disappointment at not having got something from somebody. But if the expectation itself is removed, there won't be any hurt or sorrow anymore, right?

It's impossible to quantify how much these teachings have helped me in my life.

I first took up a job at the age of 16. Finishing 12th grade in school, I was asked to join one of my siblings at work the next day. I had this habit of blindly obeying my elders; I promptly took up that job — actually a short-term job to fill my school vacation. It was in a family-managed trading company in South Bombay. I had to travel almost an hour and a half each way every day. While the working hours were from 9 am to 5 pm, my days were much longer because I was fond of cricket. I used to leave home at about 6 am for cricket practice. Finishing that, I would go to this company. I would return home late in the evening. Boy, you can imagine how tiring it must have been for me! But for almost two months, I diligently stuck to this routine. I was happy I could utilise some of my typing skills at this job, having passed my typewriting exam after my 10th grade in school.

On the one hand, I was happy to spend my time productively instead of aimlessly wandering around in the holidays. But, on the other hand, I also used to wonder why I had to slog away at a job at such a young age, when all my friends were enjoying their holidays, watching movies, playing and socialising. But the real shock was yet to come. When my vacation was coming to an end and it was time for me to leave this temporary job, I was told by this company that I wouldn't be paid for my work! This shook me badly. I thought it was unfair. I didn't know the importance of a proper appointment letter or a written contract. And I was less than 18 years old, so I was not even sure if I was even legally qualified to work. My dad and my siblings consoled me, saying it had been an opportunity for me to get some exposure to the world of work, even if I didn't get paid.

I had mixed feelings, honestly. I was terribly frustrated at having been cheated out of my wages. But at the same time, I knew that I needed to look back at life with satisfaction and gratitude, and pray that I kept doing the right thing while building my experience. I remember thinking that, the greater my struggle at that time, the greater the reward would be in future. I used this thought to propel me forward in life.

Then, when I was 17, my father got me a temporary job (for 90 days) at Life Insurance Corporation. Their office was closer to home, so commuting was easy. This is when I got some real exposure to the world of work. I could meet a number of people, and mingle with and understand the seniors in the company. I could build my network. While it restricted my freedom to wander around during the holidays, I learnt a lot about work and jobs.

While, again, my friends were having fun socialising, networking and chilling, I had to diligently reserve the time from 9 am to 5.30 pm for work every day. I learned what it takes to build one's career. I was happy that I was able to earn some money at such a young age. And I was able to fund a part of my graduate and post-graduate studies with this money. Those days, college fees weren't steep. I could also save some money to buy my clothes. Overall, that was a satisfying time for me.

Instead of looking back at any situation or decision with regret, I have always found it beneficial to look backwards with satisfaction and build confidence for the future. This mindset has, many a time, helped me think a bit more diligently about what I need to do in the future and take adequate steps for that.

After graduation, I got a job with an international corporation called Boehringer Mannheim, a pharma company, as a trainee. In those days, getting a job immediately after post-graduation was again some sort of achievement. While most middle-class youngsters like me used to study Chartered Accountancy and take up an internship in some company or another, my family's situation did not permit me this luxury. I couldn't afford to spend 3 years just earning a small stipend as an articled clerk. So I took up cost accountancy and started working as a trainee at Boehringer Mannheim. During that stint, I understood the pharma business, all about manufacturing, the various processes in a company, etc. This stint also helped me network with seniors who had completed their professional studies. Those were hard days: juggling work, study, cricket practice and the other challenges that one normally faces. I realised that I had to focus on the work at hand instead of allowing my attention to wander over several areas.

I started taking my costing studies and my career more seriously, foregoing cricket. I learned from my peers and seniors how to manage challenges and side-step constraints. I spoke to several people and understood the challenges that they had faced and the things they accomplished despite those challenges. This made me realise that life is much more — much bigger — than our day-to-day constraints.

During those early years, I learned something from my cousins too. They were slogging it out at work without adequate professional qualifications. I realised that if we wanted a thriving career, we had to have some recognised professional qualifications. I was inspired by the amount of time my cousins put in at work, and by how they managed their personal life. These little things helped me plan my time and manage my diverse interests and priorities. My cousins occasionally guided me in building my career steadily.

In the 2 or 3 years I spent at Boehringer Mannheim, I saw that there were a number of people who were very talented and innately better than me. And there were others, who, while not being so talented, had still accomplished quite a lot in life. I took these as signals of growth and the extent of the horizon that I could reach.

To shape my career, I decided to work abroad for a few years. This became an intense desire. Going abroad to work was a leap I took to avoid the rat race in India. Also, our family's hand-to-mouth existence and my father's struggle to make ends meet weighed heavily on me. I wanted to lift my family further up, financially, to compensate for whatever sacrifices my father had had to make.

I didn't want to fall behind the peers I was close to. We were a bunch of seven who used to interact closely with one other from 10th grade. It was inspiring to see their talent and the way they used to perform in academics. I was motivated to study hard and keep up with them to ensure that I don't fall out of that circle — which may have happened if I had flunked.

With all this, imagine how my father would have felt when I received the Chairman's Award at Crown Worldwide in April 2016. Coming home from the award ceremony, I handed over the crystal plaque to him and thanked him for being such an ennobling and enabling force in my life. The same goes for my mother too. Mom and Dad were probably astonished at how far I, the prankster and Grandma's pet, had come in life. Given all the struggles they had gone through to make something of their children, I am happy my parents lived through my rise in life and enjoyed every moment of it.

I cherish this feeling more than all my victories on the cricket field and in the corporate world.

Key takeaways

A growth environment is a place where your peers are ahead of you. This helps you stretch your limits. You'd better be open to being challenged continually.

Treat mistakes, frustrations, insults, failures and rejections as part of the growth process. You hardly ever achieve anything without facing these hard truths.

Listen attentively to the life experiences of the elders in your family.

Only those who risk too far can possibly find out how far one can go. – Writer T.S. Elliott

You must learn to become comfortable outside your comfort zone.

Instead of counting losses, learn to count lessons.

Where focus goes, energy flows. –Motivational speaker Tony Robbins

Please provide your views, comments, feedback and share what parts of this chapter resonates with you here

Link: https://srinivas.powervisionelectrical.co.in/chapter-2-simple-lesson-big-inspiration/

Chapter 3

Life Lessons from the Cricket Ground

Sports give you the drive to lift your competence and teach you team dynamics and group psychology on the playing field.

An overarching passion of yours can teach you a hell of a lot about work and life. Apart from giving you a deep purpose, it can reveal precious truths through its dynamics and teach you about managing behaviours when the stakes are high. Applying these lessons in the various arenas of life can lead to immense growth, as a person and as a professional.

This is what cricket did for me.

To call cricket my passion would be an understatement. It was my very life breath. Till today, I have kept a cricket ball on my table in the office. I have the habit of rolling over the seam as I dwell over possible solutions to complex problems.

Right from when I was a baby, I could sense an inexplicable bond with this game. My earliest memories of the game are of almost every adult relative of mine bringing me a gift in the form of a red ball when I was just 2 years old. They'd get me soft balls of different sizes. And my eldest uncle would replace my worn rubber balls with new ones, no questions asked. Late afternoon and late night used to be my time for rolling my arms and throwing the ball on one of the walls in our house. The constant joy of throwing the ball and catching it on the rebound is very difficult to explain. I could only experience it as a 'flow', something I am experiencing even now as I recount those memories.

We were a joint family of 6 elders and 3 children, squeezed into a one-bedroom flat measuring just 500 square feet. This home, in the Bombay suburb of Mulund, was where I spent the first 25 years of my life. News about professional cricket could only be read in the papers or heard on All India Radio. At that time, I had no inkling that cricket would be a big influence in my life; I was just immersed in the joy of playing with my toy ball!

Elders in the family loved to throw the ball to me, and I would do my best to bat with the piece of wood used for washing clothes. This piece almost resembled a cricket bat, with a nice handle suitable for my size.

One startling memory I have of that time is that I was self-centred when it came to giving my best and winning. I'd totally disregard the feelings of my friends or siblings, who too were keen to win. Much to the irritation of everyone else, I would just be focussed on winning the game instead of winning people over.

I graduated to playing with friends in my compound and then with those in our neighbourhood. And when I outgrew even them, I started going to other neighbourhoods in town, even travelling on foot at that young age, overlooking the danger of getting lost in the crowded lanes of the big city. I was driven by the sole intent of finding better pastures (read challenging opponents). Almost every building compound and lane in Mulund, where I suspected that cricket was being played, became my happy hunting ground. Slowly, I started getting invited to weekend matches and tournaments in different places.

It's fair to say that I first learnt the art of networking and making friends on those playgrounds.

When I was 11 or 12 years old, my maternal grandfather told me to get serious about life (meaning academics), saying that, if I shifted my attention from cricket to academics, I would achieve wonders. He said I could play cricket even after settling down in my career. My father backed his suggestion, adding that making inroads into professional cricket required connections with people of influence and lots of Vitamin M (money). Both these were scarce in our family. No lower-middle-class Indian family with so many dependents could afford the luxury of influence or money.

I took their suggestion seriously and started to focus on getting a decent rank in my exams to qualify for junior college and thereafter, graduate from a reputed institution. I drew up my daily schedule accordingly.

Not that I gave up cricket altogether. Just that, I reduced my play time and increased my study time. For the next few years, the theme of my life was to somehow fit cricket, along with studies, into my daily schedule.

My exposure to professional cricket started at the age of 15 when I joined Mulund College of Commerce, which was about 2.5 kilometres from my house. This college had a sound infrastructure for sports. Anyone who was serious enough to play in an inter-collegiate tournament and was disciplined enough to commit to regular practice could qualify to get into the college team. But the real challenge used to be in the inter-collegiate tournaments. For playing in these matches, we had to travel by local train, braving the heavy morning rush. It is in these matches that one learned what is called temperament.

The grounds used to be lush, the pitches were professionally prepared, and the opponent colleges boasted of their strong image (most of them were located downtown and had excellent grounds and infrastructure). Our opponent teams were familiar with the finer aspects of the game, such as the direction of the wind, the dimensions of the ground, etc. On the other hand, several of my teammates could not even afford a decent uniform comprising a shirt, trousers, shoes and socks, all white. We used to arrive at the ground wearing whatever clothes we could lay our hands on.

To forge ahead in the league, a high level of competence was paramount. But this was not easy to acquire; each member had his own set of challenges that came in the way of his preparation. Also, the degree of commitment to winning matches differed from player to player. I extrapolated this observation to everything else in life and realised that I would have to take things seriously in all walks of life if I were to achieve something big.

As far as academics were concerned, I was fortunate; most of my college friends had studied in the same school as I had and were intellectually endowed. They were God-fearing, and hailed from decent family backgrounds. They had no habit that could divert their focus from the academic path.

I spent those years developing a growth mindset and learning to focus on what I was trying to become. Except that, I was still keen to pursue cricket as a career. But I had to divide time and energy between the game and academics. I did feel constrained by time, energy and money.

In the final year of graduation, I took the bold step of switching to another college (I mentioned this in an earlier chapter): RA Podar College of Commerce & Economics. This was 15 or 20 kilometres away from my house. Every day, I had to commute by the crowded local train, travelling from Mulund to Matunga. Podar was known as the breeding ground for cricket stars. Several of those who had played on the grounds of Podar had made it to the Mumbai team in Ranji Trophy (the premier domestic first-class cricket tournament played in India between various regional teams) and eventually, to the Indian national team. I wanted to join this hallowed college to improve my game. Fortunately, I was accepted into this college, thanks to my maternal uncle's influence.

But this transition was a rude eye-opener for me; most of the team members in Podar were hard-core professional cricketers with an eye on a serious career in cricket. To get selected for the college team, you had to be among the who's who of school cricket. Unlike me, most of the players in the college team had an excellent track record in school cricket tournaments. To my deep disappointment, I realised it was too late for me to make the cut there (and therefore, in professional cricket in India). Many other players were leagues ahead of me.

Moreover, cricket in my college days taught me one unfortunate lesson: that your social status and connections mattered far more than your skills.

Sad though I was, I knew I now had to focus on studying well and building a career in the corporate world. I didn't regret the past. I was only grateful for the experiences and lessons I had gained from cricket. At Podar, I realised that many students were excellent even on the academic front — highly competent ones who had come from reputed schools in Bombay. So I had to pull up my socks if I were to have even half a chance of doing well in their midst.

I kept aside my passion for cricket and traded the desire to play on the professional level with a chance to build a solid corporate career. This was a tough call. Yet, I knew it was the right direction to pursue to make a mark in life. With my parents and most of my relatives ill-equipped to advise me on the right career path, I had to discuss this with my peers and seniors in college and do some serious introspection. I had to put my cricket kit away on the loft of our house for a few years. Every now and then, I'd take it down and look at it wistfully.

A few years later, I got a job in Hong Kong. My stint there was unremarkable from the sporting point of view, but I managed to accumulate some money to fund the international courses on Finance that I was studying. After three years in Hong Kong, I moved to Jakarta to join Crown Worldwide group. I've been with them ever since — a little more than 25 years.

And, with the move to Jakarta, cricket returned to my life in a big way.

Like I mentioned in an earlier chapter, I had the benefit of joining the International Sports Club of Indonesia (ISCI) as a member. I found that it had different types of sports, like swimming, table tennis and golf and football. The big football ground was also being used as a makeshift cricket ground for practice. What luck! Obviously, I opted to spend my time at the club playing cricket. During this time, interest in cricket began to grow in Indonesia. So I started practising diligently, braving the humid weather that sapped my energy in no time.

Just to be back on a cricket ground was bliss!

Very soon, I became the captain of the club team, purely based on my performance and attitude. And, within 2 years of getting into club cricket, I was selected for the Jakarta team to play in the regional league conducted by Indonesia Cricket Foundation. You can imagine my joy. Now, when you are leading a club successfully, it is possible that some longstanding cricket players of the club start cribbing about your appointment as captain. There could be some finger-pointing. But I learned from cricket that a team can have people of different backgrounds, profiles and attitudes. We should not get bogged down by these things on a personal level. We should only be concerned about getting the best out of each player and winning matches for the club, region or nation we are representing.

We lifted some annual league trophies in Jakarta, which saw me get into the Indonesia national team in 2005. And again in 2007.

My experiences in the practice sessions and matches gave me some important perspectives on what it takes to succeed in bigger things in life. Firstly, I learned that you must work hard to improve from one level to the next. You have to improve your mindset, commitment, performance and energy, and the ability to withstand rumourmongers and those who don't like your progress. And you should improve on all this *fast*!

Then, playing cricket at so many venues in so many teams against so many opponent teams in so many tournaments helped me take the initiative and raise my hand whenever I was needed, either as an administrator or as a player. This also taught me when to attack, when to defend, and how to add value to the team (especially when things were in disarray), when to remain on the sidelines, how to handle disruptions, etc.

Above all, I learnt to focus on *winning matches*. This gave me a winner's attitude in other areas of life too, especially my career. I have implemented the lessons learned on the cricket field in the corporate world and enjoyed a vibrant career so far. I have handled situations of every kind, turned around my company in Jakarta and India, tided over complications and confrontations peacefully, helped my team members grow along with me ... the things I've been able to do because of cricket are so many. Indeed, the game has been a friend, philosopher, and guide to me.

The most crucial lesson I've learned on the cricket ground is that I must be a great leader for my team, regardless of whether I hold a formal position of authority (like Captain) or not. I have to lead them to victory.

On exercising leadership

Link 1: https://youtu.be/xxzBtpaNx2U
Duration: 00:35 Mts.

On exercising leadership: Be the leader of your Life. Lead yourself where you want to be. Breathe life back into your ambitions, your desires, your goals, your relationship. What we achieve internally will be reflected in our outer reality. We don't need a title for that. It is within our own ambit.

It doesn't matter who or how a person is, as long as we can bring several people and artfully combine their positive traits to build a winning team. This is what matters in life. This is something I implemented successfully even at work, and continue to do so even today, thanks largely to the freedom allowed by my organisation.

No matter how bad the situation is, we need a positive attitude to score a winning proposition — whether in cricket, any other game, or for that matter, any other walk of life.

Key takeaways

Learn the art of building your network at the earliest. It will be useful for life.

Be prepared to shift gears from passion to profession, but be wary of putting off the pursuit of passion forever. When it comes to pursuing your passion, make the most out of every opportunity once you are reasonably settled in life, instead of deferring it to a later date.

The difference between ordinary and extraordinary is that little extra.

To know more about the world, we need to do things we have never done before.

The habit of winning, once gained in one walk of life, can be replicated in other walks of life as well.

Words of wisdom from elders have their own merits.

Try to be a rainbow in someone's cloud. – Writer Maya Angelou

Please provide your views, comments, feedback and share what parts of this chapter resonates with you here

Link: https://srinivas.powervisionelectrical.co.in/chapter-3-life-lesson-from-the-cricket-ground/

Chapter 4

New Ways to Learn

If knowledge is power, then learning is a super power. Our capacity to learn is limitless. We simply need to be shown how to *access* this capacity. Today we see a number of reliable methods and practical tools to enhance our learning. But I learned a lot through the simple tried and tested method of heeding my parents' suggestions.

The current generation of youngsters has the opportunity to give feedback to their teachers and help them course-correct whenever required.

This 2-way communication loop, I believe, enhances learning and is good for everybody concerned.

When I did my primary schooling, I was made to believe that the seeds of our intellect are determined by the grace and good wishes of the soul, which bestows knowledge irrespective of age, gender, background or ethnicity.

I learn spiritual music from someone who is younger than me but who has been practising it for more than 25 years. Needless to say, he is my master in this subject. And I am a student, learning and imbibing with due respect whatever he teaches me. My master calls it 'the power of intent'.

In a rapidly changing world where one has to continuously unlearn, learn and relearn, the right rules of encouragement and the unconditional support of a master are preconditions for students of life. We should just ensure that we develop a mind that is always open to learning.

Learning new things regularly

Link 1: https://youtu.be/l8yrHVA48nM
Duration: 00:41 Mts.

> One of the signs of progress in life is to find out what is it new that we have learnt in today's order of disruption. We need to continuously keep learning and educate ourselves because as Robin says Learning and Education are inoculation against disruption otherwise life gets boring to be within the limits of what you know.

We have to find a way to apply whatever we learn from our teacher, master, lecturer or anybody else who takes up the role of a coach in some form or the other. Also, to attain true mastery in a subject, we have to tap diverse sources of knowledge in that subject.

In this VUCA (vulnerable, uncertain, complex, ambiguous) world, it is essential to develop a culture of applied learning through rigorous practice. You're likely to commit mistakes. But this is the only way to become different in this commoditised world, where almost everyone follows a straitjacketed way to apply what they learn in a classroom. And then they wonder why they fail!

On applying knowledge and ideas

Link 2: https://youtu.be/QwIysHykx6Y
Duration: 01:09 Mts.

> On application of knowledge and ideas: Knowing and doing are two different things. We must learn new things and gather knowledge. We must generate ideas by talking to others, however, we must also apply them. Willingness alone is not enough; we must do it. Big ideas remain superficial unless we find a useful way to apply it. This might seem quite daunting and strange. But if you want to be an elite performer, you should do strange things. Initially, this might be hard, but as you make it a ritual, it becomes second nature. We have to find a way to convert superficiality into granularity by applying our awareness for impactful results. This is one of the secrets of uber-successful people. Do you want to be one?

Remember, technology is only a tool to expedite our learning by giving us better access to sources of knowledge and improving our learning timelines.

We tend to believe that we're always right in our opinions and beliefs. Our strong preconceived notions blind us to the truth. For example, we feel that by learning a subject we know everything about it, including what others should understand.

We only see what we want to see. We only hear what we want to hear. Our belief system is like a mirror; it shows us only what we believe. Or like an echo chamber; it merely bounces our thoughts back to us. This can be seen in a variety of scenarios every day.

For example, when I speak English, my accent and pronunciation may not be correct. I may pause a number of times in the course of my conversations. My grammar may be wrong. So this can create a chamber of thought in my mind, in which my belief (that my English is not good enough) keeps echoing. Other ideas and beliefs, including the one that I can improve my English, are dismissed. This leads to a limiting belief about my capability. I'd best avoid this.

I can improve my English by joining a language training course. Similarly, if I want to improve my oratory skills, I can do that by joining a speaking club. In fact, I actually *did* join the Toastmasters Club to become an effective public speaker.

It is important to recognise that our beliefs do not necessarily always reflect reality. So being cognisant of one's biases and trying to be open to constructive criticism can help us overcome our limiting beliefs, enhance our learning, expand our horizons and improve. This has helped me in several ways, especially in talking to prospects and customers.

Now, each one of us has an unlimited capacity to learn in different ways and should be careful to not stick to just one style.

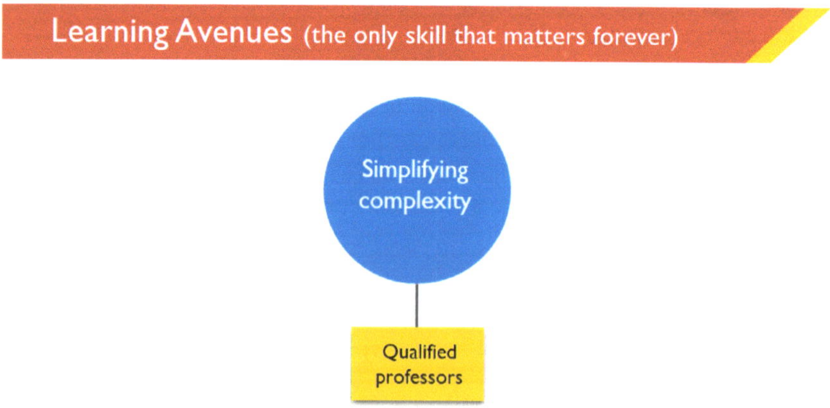

Learn, unlearn & relearn for growth mindset

In this era of Zoom and online learning, visual learning is one of the important ways. When I was doing my MBA at Chicago Booth Business School, their Singapore campus used to relay lectures online. I saw professors converting almost 50 pages of complex information into just 5 impactful Power Point slides! This made it so easy for us students to understand what was being taught. Similarly, when I had to make presentations, I tried to express my ideas the same way.

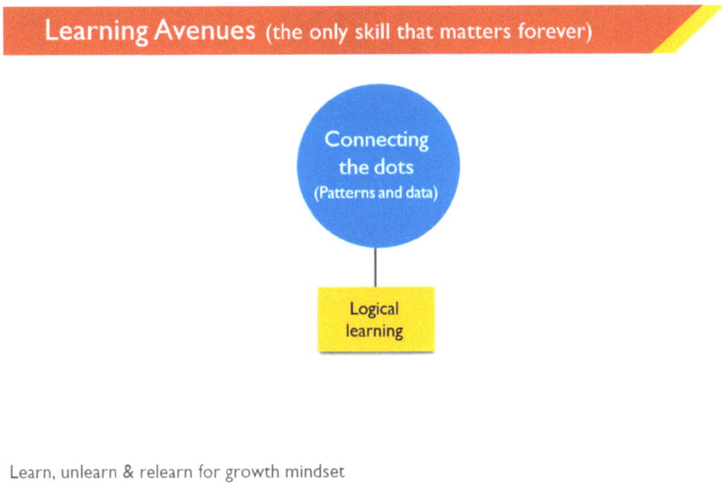

Another learning style is logical learning — looking at patterns and data and solving problems or expressing thoughts by connecting the dots. This is what I adopted as an internal auditor at Crown Worldwide Group between 2004 and 2009. This made data-driven decision-making easy.

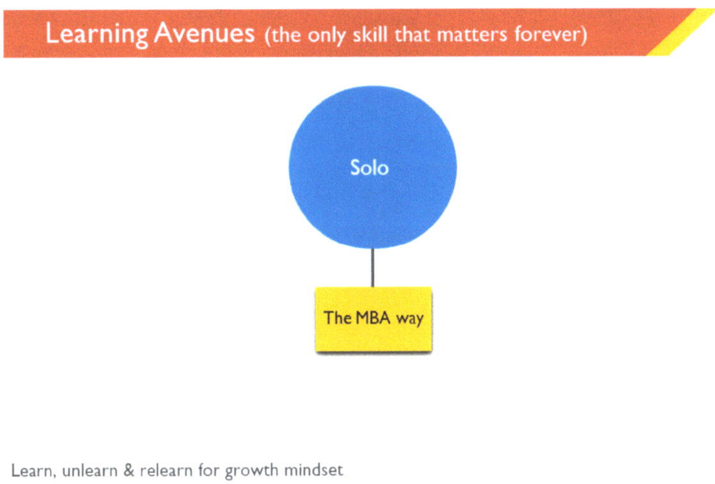

Solo learning is yet another learning style. This is usually practised by great thought leaders and visionaries, who reflect through their journals every day. This method was used even in the MBA program I referred to earlier. I could see the solo learners among us students express themselves with reference to what they had learned when they were alone. It was very nice to see them paraphrasing their learning. This was especially useful to those in remote countries, who did not have access to different learning mechanisms.

Learning Avenues (the only skill that matters forever)

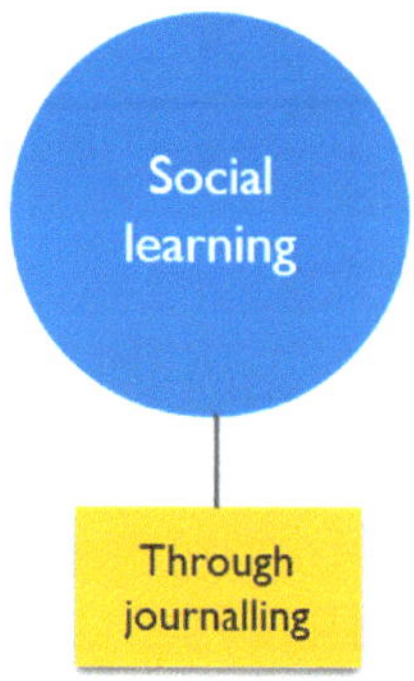

Learn, unlearn & relearn for growth mindset

The fourth type of learning is social learning. For instance, in the same class, many of my European and American friends never used to touch their class notes. They used to just listen to our professors closely and be attentive during the peer learning sessions. They used to enjoy the social interactions and hands-on activities in class. And then, they would present concepts and thoughts as great storytellers the next day. So you don't have to be only reading books to be a learner; you can learn socially as well.

Learning Avenues (the only skill that matters forever)

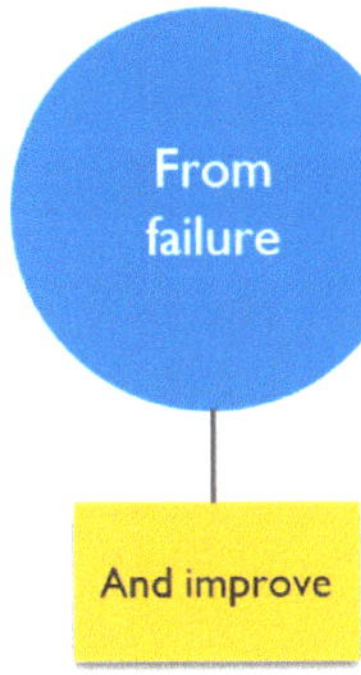

Learn, unlearn & relearn for growth mindset

Everybody likes to win. Most of us also like to believe that if we don't always win, we will be called under-achievers, or even failures. We've been taught to think from a very early age that winning is everything, and failure is to be avoided at all costs.

But I have learned from the school of life that this is so wrong. We need to understand that winning isn't everything. We can't always win, and this is ok too. But what is critical is to take failure in our stride and never to give up. We must learn from our failures and improve ourselves on the path to success.

Let's accept it, failure, as much as it hurts, is part and parcel of life. Despite all our talent, skills and knowledge, it is inevitable that we will fail from time to time. The current generation has to come to terms with this crucial fact of life to avoid ending up in depression and taking some unfortunate steps.

Failure has two sides: one that makes you strong and another that leaves you skeptical. I have always benefited from embracing the former. For instance, take my transfer from Jakarta to Bombay in Crown Worldwide. When my first attempt to get transferred to Bombay (in 2002) failed, I enrolled in the MBA program at Chicago Booth Business School, resolving to become a better, more rounded, professional. I paid a fortune for this course, but it paid me back handsomely.

Similarly, I got another opportunity to return to India in 2006. This time, I was to head the India operations of Crown. I had sent my family ahead and was on the verge to moving to Bombay myself when I was given the sad news that the transfer was not going to happen. It was like being struck by a bolt of lightning! But I took even this in my stride and bided my time in Jakarta, continuing to do my best at work and constantly grooming myself for a very senior role in the company.

And when I finally did get transferred to Bombay in 2010, eight years after my first attempt, I was absolutely ready for the new role and the stiff challenges that came with it. I was able to turn around the performance of the company in India and take it to new heights. Even on the cricket ground, it was after stumbling and falling repeatedly that I made it to the big level.

History is replete with instances of successful people from every walk of life — politics, business, sports, etc. — who tasted success only after failing several times. In fact, they used the failures to turn their lives around.

So, if you have encountered failure at some point, I suggest you stop worrying. Because you are in the incredible company of several stalwarts and can learn from them.

One of the best reasons to fail sometimes is the fact that you learn more from failure and setbacks than from all the quick successes you might have had.

On learning, living, loving, and growing

Link 3: https://youtu.be/1ziJDTekqmY
Duration: 01:27 Mts.

> On learning, living, loving and growing: Mistakes help us to grow, failures help us to keep learning, hopes help us to keep going, and loving is the reason we are all here. So just keep learning, living, loving and growing.

In fact, in interviews for leadership positions, questions are asked about the candidate's failures, how they overcame those failures and what they learned from them.

I have learned that the only true failure in life is to not try.

If we're used to being the best, we might not be able to empathise with those who aren't (the best). This can cause us to be insensitive, but we may not realise it. But when we are considerate to others, we are likely to be more involved in helping them, as we can better relate to their situation. Being humble is something many of us struggle with, but it is an important characteristic of a good leader. And if you've learned it from your own life, nothing like it!

Learning Avenues (the only skill that matters forever)

Learn, unlearn & relearn for growth mindset

Learning on the go

It was in 2015 that I first participated in a half-marathon. I knew nothing about the effort and preparation needed. On the day of the marathon, when I reached the venue, I saw thousands of people warming up and preparing themselves for the run! What an amazing sight!

Similarly, I didn't know the right attire for such a run. I was wearing a shoe with a sharp top; sure to hurt my toes. When the race started, I just went along with the crowd. I somehow finished the race with great difficulty. But I was determined that 5 years from then, I would run a full marathon.

As part of my preparation, I joined a fitness club called Club Marathon and started practising with the other members. I learned to increase my energy and capacity enough to run a full marathon. And in 2020, just before the Covid-19 pandemic struck, I registered for my first full marathon — in Bombay.

But even then, I hadn't fully prepared for a marathon. The longest stretch I had run was 26 kilometres. Predictably, on race day, I started tiring after the 26 km mark. Still, I imbibed the energy and motivation of my fellow runners and pushed myself to the hilt. And finally, I managed to complete the marathon! It was excruciatingly difficult, but the big thing is that I did manage to finish the race, and within the time limit for my age — a big leap for me. All thanks to my learning on the go, from my ecosystem of runners. Learning on the go is one of the core tenets of improving your personal brand.

Learning Avenues (the only skill that matters forever)

Learn, unlearn & relearn for growth mindset

All of us can learn a lot by being good listeners. Now, while I've had a problem articulating my thoughts by speaking (maybe because of lack of confidence), I have always been a good listener. If you want to go deep into the art and benefits of listening, read the book *Deep Listening: Impact Beyond Words* by Oscar Trimboli.

It was only somewhat late in life that I realised that listening is a skill. It's a practice, and a way to balance how we communicate. Most of us think that by talking more, talking faster and talking energetically, we become better communicators. You'll see this behaviour in classrooms, corporate meetings and everywhere else. Nothing can be further from the truth.

Great communicators are great listeners too. Great listeners demonstrate curiosity, flexibility and openness. And as we keep going up the hierarchy in any organisation, we realise that listening matters more and more.

It has been found that a human being can talk at an average speed of 125 words per minute. But they can listen to 400 words per minute and think at the rate of 900 words per minute. Doesn't this tell us how much more important listening and thinking are than talking?

In any conversation, when we want to learn something, we must listen intently. And breathe slowly and deeply. Because the deeper we breath, the deeper we listen and the better we think. This has been proven scientifically. We need to listen with our whole body, not just with our ears.

Taking notes is also part of the listening process. Remember, 'silent' and 'listen' are made up of the same letters. When we listen deeply, opposing ideas and views can co-exist peacefully.

In this era of digitisation, it would be incomplete to talk about learning without talking about focus. Check out Jim Kwik's book *Limitless*. He suffered brain damage from an injury during his childhood. When he grew up, he did some deep research and come out with a strategy to cope with the always-on digital culture and to learn even in this milieu.

Learning Avenues (the only skill that matters forever)

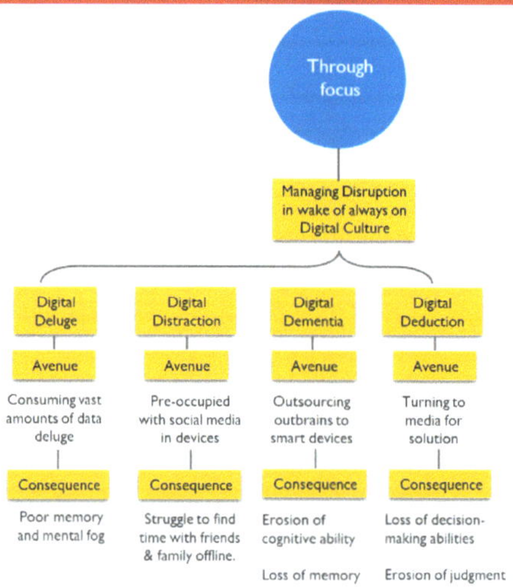

Learn, unlearn & relearn for growth mindset

Jim talks about four important concepts: digital deluge, digital distraction, digital dementia and digital deduction.

Digital deluge. We have unfettered access to mountains of information from several sources online. So we consume a vast amount of data every day. Most of us have got too much to process in a limited time; we are overwhelmed. There is a growing body of evidence which suggests that if we never let our mind wander or be idle, and always keep it engaged in consuming information, we will pay a price in the form of poor memory, mental fog and fatigue. Indeed, this is already happening to several people, possibly even to you.

Next, he talks about **Digital distraction**. We are always connected to digital devices and media. We, therefore, struggle to find the time to be with our families and friends offline. And even when we are with them, our minds and eyes are often on a digital screen. We find it difficult to establish a genuine connection with people. In spite of being physically present, we are not *available* to them. We are preoccupied with scrolling through our social media feeds, reading emails, checking WhatsApp messages, etc. And even at work, we struggle to stay focussed.

The fallacy of multi-tasking

Link 4: https://youtu.be/F8RprRWwC7w
Duration: 01:29 Mts.

Today we will talk about the fallacy of multitasking. In the past, a person's capability to do several tasks in record time used to be applauded and credited. In an automated world today, we have to be ensuring that we give respect to the act of focusing on single thing at a time. In a digital

> world, where gadgets have become affordable and accessible, there is always a tendency to do several things at the same time. However, our mind gets habituated to distraction and in a commoditized world, if anything which is respected today, it is human intelligence. And human intelligence which can bring out any idea worthy of execution requires what Robin Sharma called as the 'tight bubble of total focus'. Research has proven time and again that unless you focus on one thing at a time you are no different from others. Try to focus, pay respect to attention as an important element of your trait and you'll see the difference. This requires you to be developing a habit of not multitasking.

We look forward to the dopamine hits we get from the likes, comments and shares we receive on social media, and from the messages we get from various people. This further reinforces our digitally distracted behaviour.

We don't realise it, but this behaviour is rewiring our brains for the worse. It is diminishing our ability to concentrate on any one thing, prioritise the important over the trivial and deeply engage with important content.

Researcher Ryan Dyer from the University of Columbia, through a study, showed how digital habits are affecting relationships. In an experiment, more than 300 adults, including university students, were asked to keep their phones on a table where they were easily accessible to them. Another set of people was asked to put the phones in 'silent' mode and keep them in a container on the table. And then both groups were asked to have a meal.

Afterwards, participants were asked to respond to questions about their feelings of connectedness, enjoyment, distraction and boredom during the meal.

Those whose phones were accessible used them more often. They described themselves as feeling more distracted during the meal. They also enjoyed the dinner less than those who had put their phones into the container.

Modern technology may be wonderful, but it can easily sidetrack us and take away special moments — *important* moments — in life.

Next, Jim Kwik talks about **Digital dementia** in his book.

When is the last time you had to remember someone's phone number? What about the numbers of the people you talk to, or text, every day?

When I was young, one had to remember one's friends' phone numbers. But you no longer have to do this, right? Because your mobile phone remembers them for you. This is not to say that should carry in your head all the numbers on your phone. But it is a fact that we have lost our ability to remember more than one or two phone numbers. Heck, we can't even remember some of the conversations we had yesterday, or what transpired a week ago!

It's the same with GPS. When we want to find the route to a place, we immediately check Google Maps. Forgotten is the habit of asking locals to guide us and then relying on our memory and instinct to follow their directions.

This is digital dementia: an erosion of our cognitive abilities and memory due to the overuse of digital technology. Neuroscientist Manfred Spitzer was the first to use the term 'digital dementia' in this context.

Thankfully, even today, I switch off my phone during meetings to pay full attention to what's going on. And after every meeting, I try to recollect the highlights manually and jot them down in a notepad.

Maria Wimber of the University of Birmingham told BBC that this habit of looking up information on digital media and devices — this over-reliance — prevents the development of our long-term memory. Another study says that the brain is more like a muscle; the more we use it, the stronger and better it gets. So the more it can store and the better it can work.

But too often, we outsource our brains to our 'smart' devices. And these 'smart' devices are, well, making us a little stupider with each passing day.

Finally, we come to **Digital deduction**. In a digital-first world, millions of us, especially youngsters, try to obtain the answer to any question or problem with the click of the mouse or the swipe of a finger. We are relying less and less on our memory, knowledge and analytical abilities. This leads to over-confidence, while eroding our judgment, instinct and decision-making abilities.

Instead, what if we built our capacity to analyse, deduce and infer?

There are ways to do this. I strongly recommend that you read *Limitless*.

Learning Avenues (the only skill that matters forever)

Learn, unlearn & relearn for growth mindset

From the time I started playing cricket, in my teens, I have had this habit of keeping myself fit by running or exercising in a gym. Research has proven the powerful beneficial effects of exercise on the brain and our health, and our ability to respond to complex situations. It's essential therefore to find the time to exercise every day. Dr. John J Ratey, an Associate Clinical Professor of Psychology at Harvard Medical School, says in his book *Spark – The Revolutionary New Science of Exercise and the Brain* that exercise is a medicine. Research has also established the body-mind-body connection: meaning, our body has an influence on our mind, and vice versa.

Exercise is a growth stock. It is the best way to stay healthy, alert and happy. Working out regularly can help build a better, nimbler brain. I have found that every time I come back from a long run, I can do the most complex of tasks more easily than otherwise. I think exercise gives us the fuel to address problems and situations and come up with good, workable solutions.

Physical activity during exercise sparks biological changes that encourage our brain cells to bind to one another. For the brain to learn, these connections must be made. They reflect the brain's fundamental ability to adapt to challenges. I have found that exercise provides an unparalleled stimulus to the brain. The brain is willing and able to learn. I have experienced this since my college days.

Also, exercise sharpens our awareness of ourselves and our surroundings. On most of the days that I exercise, I'm more alert and aware. Among other things, this is the best antidote to a cranky attitude. So much so, that in Western countries, students schedule their hardest subjects immediately after their workouts to capitalise on the beneficial effects of exercise.

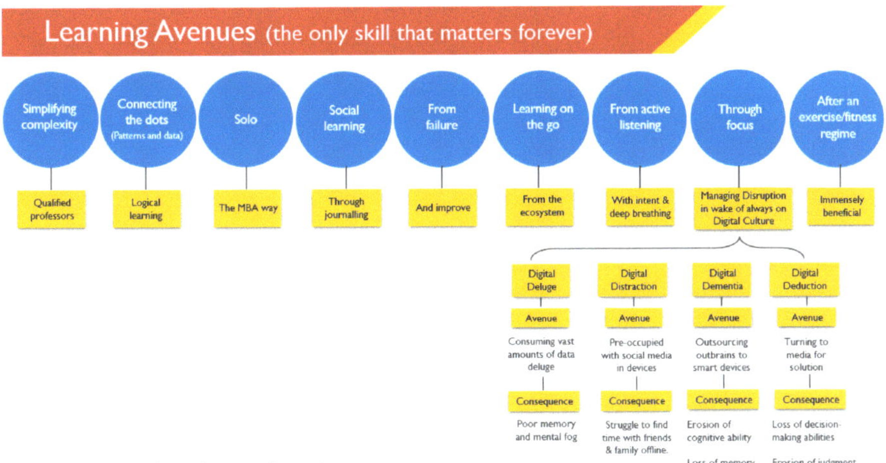

Learn, unlearn & relearn for growth mindset

Key takeaways

Don't rely solely on your employer for your career growth; learning, unlearning and relearning are the only pathways to one's growth.

There are different ways of adding to your knowledge toolkit. Stretch yourself to acccss these.

Learn to avoid the digital traps (digital deluge, digital distraction, digital dementia and digital deduction).

Improve your learning ability through regular exercise in some form. Consistent fitness is the key to energising oneself continuously.

Please provide your views, comments, feedback and share what parts of this chapter resonates with you here

Link: https://srinivas.powervisionelectrical.co.in/chapter-4-new-ways-to-learn/

Chapter 5

Moving Away from the Rat Race

It is said that the world is a book. And if you've not travelled, you've read just one page of the book.

Before going to Hong Kong in 1994, I worked in India between 1989 and 1994. I worked as a trainee and then as Assistant Manager – Costing with Boehringer Mannheim, a pharmaceutical company.

I then moved to another pharmaceutical company, Merind (which belonged to the Tata group), as Assistant Manager – Finance. Shifting from Costing to Finance was more of a political hurdle. One reason I moved from a cosy and comfortable Boehringer to Merind, despite knowing that I'd have to tolerate a long commute every day, was that Merind was in the vicinity of several five-star hotels and a few recruitment firms. This made it easy for me to meet representatives of the recruitment firms and attend interviews at lunch time and after work in the evening. I had set my sights on going abroad for work. So, while I took my stints at Boehringer and Merind seriously and did my best, I saw these jobs as stepping stones to my stint abroad.

The Boehringer office was in Andheri, a distant suburb of Bombay, whereas Merind's office was in downtown Colaba. In those days, several Indians with work experience of 3 or 4 years were going to the Middle East to work, attracted by the higher salaries and the zero-tax regime. This was especially true of Finance and Administration executives. But, after learning that the Middle East was hot and humid for most of the year, I wasn't keen to go there. (Due respect, though, to my friends and relatives who have settled there, occupying key positions for many years.)

Also, I was fond of nature, and the Middle East had little to offer by way of natural beauty. Wherever I lived, I wanted to go out and enjoy the weather, the view of the sky and other natural attractions. Deep down, I also think I just wanted to be different from most others — not be part of a herd. (My due respects again to those who have moved to the Middle East to make a living. To each their own; I'm just narrating my personal point of view and experiences here).

So, when I got to know that there were a number of job opportunities in Hong Kong and Singapore, I zeroed in on the former. I got in touch with an employment agency in South Bombay. They didn't have an immediate opening in Hong Kong, so I kept in regular touch with the manager of the agency. Finally, he gave me the opportunity to attend an interview with a company for a role in that country. The interview was pretty formal. I was straightforward, and didn't try to mix words or exaggerate stuff about myself. I was quite frank about my background.

To my good fortune, I was selected for that position. The fact that Hong Kong was a British colony helped. I wanted to do CIMA (Chartered Institute of Management Accountants, headquartered in UK), a prestigious course that would fast-track my career. I was fascinated by the CIMA curriculum. In Hong Kong, I could earn in dollars, which would help me fund this course.

Hong Kong seemed the perfect place for me to hunker down and take up CIMA. I went there in April 1994, at the age of 26. I left in 1997, when the country was being handed over formally by the UK to China.

In going to Hong Kong, I travelled abroad for the first time. I did not even know that I had to cross the immigration counter at the airport if I wanted to go abroad. It was only after crossing the immigration desk at Bombay airport that reality started dawning on me: I was going to be living all alone for God only knew how many years. I was anxious, frightened and sad, but I knew that there was no turning back; I was going abroad for a very important reason.

When I reached Hong Kong, I found the weather to be relatively cold vis-à-vis Bombay. Those days, there was no internet to inform you about the weather in any place. Although I had a sweater and a Pathani coat, I found the 13-degree Celsius temperature too cold for my comfort.

It was not easy to cross the immigration desk at Hong Kong airport because it looked as it people of my ethnicity were less preferred over there; and the desk happened to be manned by someone who seemed to be of a different origin. He grilled me for almost 45 minutes before giving me a 'visa on arrival' for 3 months.

I began to realise that life was going to be completely different in Hong Kong from what I was used to in India. Back at home, I had been a pampered lad. My mother wouldn't even allow me to heat water! Not that I took an interest in the household chores. My mother was completely dedicated to our family's requirements and took care of everything. And I'd just study, play and do whatever else lads of my age did.

The first few months in Hong Kong were gruelling. First of all, a Hong Kong dollar was worth almost 5.5 Indian rupees. Everything seemed expensive to me. And the weather was different, the people were different. They were not all that friendly. Then, finding vegetarian food was like finding water in a desert; only about one in a hundred restaurants served it. And half of those served boiled vegetables that only a monk would eat. As a result, vegetarian food that was even half-edible was damn expensive! I found it as a cultural shock over the fact that the whole population was eating meat of some type or the other, including snakes and insects. This shook me. It took a while for me to reconcile to the fact that I had to somehow tolerate that kind of a place for a few years. I had made a 'gentleman's commitment' to the company I had joined that I would work there for at least 3 years.

All in all, Hong Kong was a culture shock for me.

Almost every day was difficult. I had to walk and take a train on my way to work and back home. A fellow Indian colleague of mine used to scare me by warning me that it was not easy to live in that country. Luckily, I soon got hold of another Indian who came to render software services to the company I was working for. He was easy to talk to. I found out that he was in need of a flat mate for his rented apartment; I agreed to become that roommate. Leaving my shanty dwelling in central Hong Kong, where I had been staying thus far (opposite the prison, no less), I took up digs with this person.

Once I settled down there, I enrolled myself in the CIMA course. This course exposed me to the world of international business, something Indian courses did not. My goal was to complete this course and look for a job in a multinational corporation. I could thus get a head start over my peers and uplift my family financially.

My dad had retired about 4 years earlier. He had spent a large part of his savings on the weddings of my two sisters. He was now left with only his provident fund. I did not want to depend on him financially. On the contrary, I wanted to support my parents by sending them money regularly. I knew that if I had continued to work in India, I would never be able to do that — let alone buy my own house and elevate my standard of living.

To be honest, I left India for another (sneaky) reason too: to escape Dad's repeated demand that I get married, even though I was just 26! Marriage would have been too much of a responsibility for me at that point in time.

In Hong Kong, I worked for an export finance company. They used to import a number of items from China and export a number of items to Africa. I got comfortable with the type of business they were doing, though not with some of their work practices.

After a year or so, I moved out of the apartment I mentioned and started living in a place closer to my office. I could now find more time to study the Chartered Financial Analyst course, which I had joined in India, and the CIMA course.

Life was not comfortable. Since I could not afford to eat in a restaurant, I had to learn to cook. I purchased all the vessels and started cooking my daily meals. I was fortunate that my roommate helped me and shared the initiative to cook.

I kept telling myself that I would find the first available opportunity to move out of Hong Kong when I finished my 3-year stint in that company. Because the culture there was not all that friendly towards people of other ethnicities, especially those from South Asia. It was not easy to deal with the people of Hong Kong. Being a person of frank nature, I found it difficult to keep my opinions to myself, which was what I was asked to do.

I had to do everything in the house myself: washing my clothes, cooking breakfast, lunch and dinner, keeping the flat clean. In the evening, I used to come home at 7 pm, cook my dinner, eat it and then stay up till 10.30 or 11 pm, studying. Remember, I was contending with not one course but two! And in those days, there was no internet, so no online help. I could only read the books and go through the study plan.

Initially, it was quite frustrating. But I learned to organise myself and my day, and become more independent and responsible. I couldn't afford to even forget the key to my house! (One day, I did forget it at home and had to request my landlord to come over to open it with his spare key. He was kind enough to do so.)

I met many people from different ethnicities and nationalities. It was incredible to see so many people from places like Sri Lanka, Bangladesh and Pakistan, in addition to different parts of India, make a living in Hong Kong. I got to know their lifestyles and their backgrounds. Some of them had the courage to leave their jobs and start their own businesses with little or no capital. It taught me that there is no one way to lead your life.

There is a difference between coming up in life on your mettle and being served everything on a platter. More than 65% or 70% of the Asian population is below the age of 45. While we hear a lot about the easy-going nature of millennials, it is not their fault. Because they don't have to struggle to come up in life, unlike their predecessors (including their parents). Today, everything is available at their fingertips, especially information. Their college education is paid for by their parents. Many of them go abroad for higher studies. And they can choose from a multitude of career streams. Because of the information deluge, they feel they know everything. However, this deluge is diminishing their thinking power — their processing power. And their power to find solutions to difficult problems (I've touched upon this in the chapter on new ways of learning).

And so, I am afraid they're going to find it pretty hard when things get tough. We already hear a lot of things about mental health, depression, suicide, the need for therapy, etc. in youngsters. Many of them are not finding it easy to keep going in life. An acute shortage of psychologists and counsellors is likely to crop up in the near future.

Youngsters must learn to be on their toes continuously to adapt to the changes in the ecosystem. A permanent job is almost a dream now. The job stability and security that my generation used to enjoy are almost non-existent. Almost all companies are facing tough times due to heavy competition and the commodification of almost everything in the market. Youngsters therefore need to be agile enough to find different avenues of income and keep learning new things. Only then can they move on and make a mark in life.

Returning to my Hong Kong story, after keeping my commitment to working for three years with my then-employer, I joined Crown Worldwide Group in Jakarta. Moving from Hong Kong, which was growing at a breathtaking speed and was economically quite developed, to Indonesia, which, though growing fast, was economically far behind, was tough. I felt I was getting demoted in life, but I was determined to find my own space and a way to grow.

My fears about Jakarta turned out to be unfounded. It was a fascinating place! Its people were friendly, mild, humble and welcoming. They respected Indians (probably because most Indonesians are actually of Indian origin. They were converted to Islam by Arab traders and invaders when they moved from South India to Indonesia and its neighbouring countries for the spice trade.)

But economically speaking, it was a deeply troubling time. It was September 1997 when I moved to Jakarta. The Asian financial crisis hit the world just then; most Asian currencies were getting heavily devalued. The Indonesian Rupiah was 2,440 to a US Dollar, and the day I reached Jakarta, I was told that it got further devalued by 300 Rupiah. Moreover, Indonesia was an autocratic nation. The president, Suharto, ran it like his fiefdom. Nepotism, corruption, collusion and what not were rampant. The bottom line? There was a crisis and people started leaving the place in droves.

This proved providential for my company, Crown Worldwide.

Since we were (and are) in the business of helping people relocate, our business began to take off! Many people leaving Indonesia used to just hand over their keys to us and ask us to pack their goods and ship them to wherever they were headed. So, business-wise, it was a fantastic time for us.

And since I had been sent from the corporate headquarters in Hong Kong to handle the company's finances and ensure proper governance in Indonesia, I could implement some systems, processes and controls. That proved to be the turning point of my career. And the turning point of Crown's business in Indonesia. From being almost nowhere in the group's global network, we started making a mark. And in two years of my being there, we became No. 3 or No. 4 in the group!

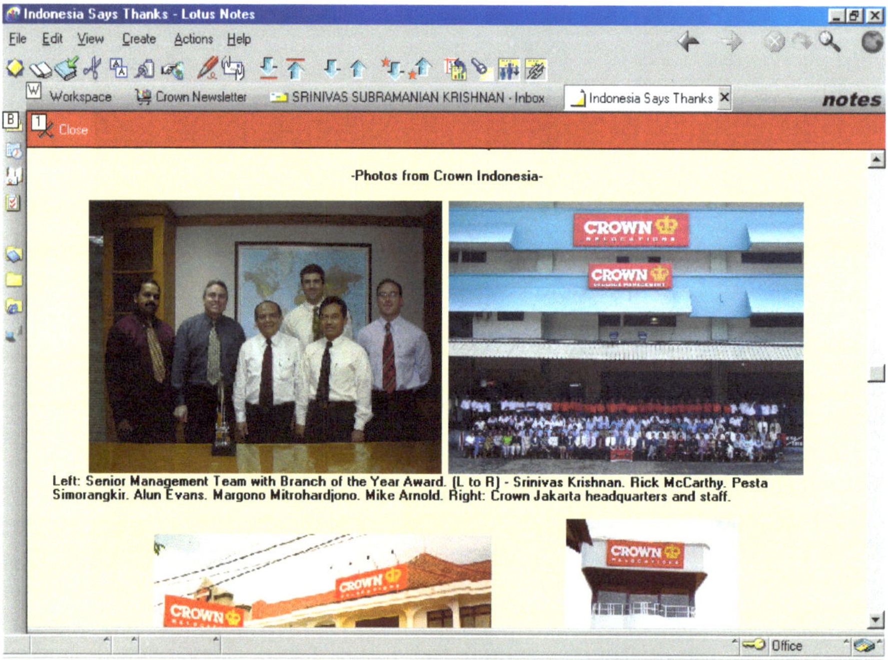

Indonesia proved to be a dramatic turning point in my personal life too. It was soon after I joined the Jakarta office of Crown that I got married — in January 1998. My wife Jayashree moved in with me and we started our life in Indonesia. My cricketing career too took off there, as I explain in other chapters. So, in several ways, that was a momentous period in my life.

Had I not taken up that job, fearing what kind of country Indonesia was or because I thought I could not get used to living there, I would have missed out on these big opportunities for professional and personal growth. There is simply no substitute for gaining experience in the field. As John Le Carre said, 'A desk is a dangerous place from which to view the world.'

Even after his retirement (in 1990, I think), my father was quite healthy and agile. He kept himself busy by taking up some small work assignment or the other. But after my brother and I moved out of Bombay, my parents were all alone. Though they visited my brother in Hong Kong, my sister in the USA and me in Jakarta every quarter, they were by themselves in Bombay during the festival season. Their health started worsening, given their advancing age. I could see a steady deterioration in their health from the year 2000 to 2008. Even Jayashree's dad's health was deteriorating (she lost her mom in 2002).

That is when we decided to move back to India and be close to our parents for the rest of their lives.

Going from Jakarta to Bombay was neither cheap nor easy. Our lifestyle had to be revamped because the infrastructure and facilities we enjoyed in Indonesia were not available to us in Bombay. Firstly, we were moving from a mansion in Jakarta to the 1.5-bedroom flat we owned in Bombay. Since we had to be close to my parents, we stayed in a flat on the floor above them. Secondly, Bombay was cramped, crowded and polluted. Though it had been all this even when I left India in 1994, I thought the living conditions had worsened in the intervening 16 years. The decade of growth from 2000 to 2010 had changed a lot in terms of the attitude and approach of the people, the city's infrastructure, etc. I realised that rapid economic growth of a nation, leaving social growth behind, is not always pleasant. Thirdly, I could see a change in the behaviour of some of our acquaintances towards us, when we returned to Bombay for good. So overall, it was difficult to live in this city.

In Jakarta, my children used to have separate rooms in our house. Whereas in Bombay, they had to fit themselves into a small room. And then, in Indonesia, we were staying in an independent house. Whereas in Bombay, we had to climb 3 floors in a building that didn't have an elevator. Every monsoon, the traffic jams and the flooding of the roads used to wreak havoc in our lives. Life in Bombay is always rushed, we found, unlike in Jakarta.

More than my children and me, my wife Jayashree had to grapple with the new conditions. She was running a family in the city, making sure that the children were sent to school on time with proper food and that their studies were also being attended to. Generally speaking, we had to live with a degree of commotion in our lives. The only major consolation for us was that, apart from being close to our parents, we could meet our relatives and friends more often than before.

But we did take these drastic changes in our stride. We simply had to, to keep moving ahead. In the next few years, dad's health went up and down. He had to be frequently treated for some illness or the other. Sometimes, he had to be hospitalised. I was fortunate to have the support of my uncle, his two brothers and my aunts, who lived in the same suburb as we did.

Jayashree too did a lot of heavy lifting. In fact, she was the lynchpin of our family.

In October 2016, dad eventually passed on.

Ah, well. In a sense, my life came full circle when I found myself back in my home city of Bombay, 16 years after I left it in search of greener professional pastures. India had gone through a spurt of growth when we had been away. We missed watching the country experience above-average growth for more than a decade.

Brand Ambassador of India 2013

And, as a company, we at Crown could probably have done much better in India. But, for whatever reason, almost everything was going wrong in the company when I took charge of its India operations and returned to Bombay. But I'm grateful that I could leverage my experience of working abroad, my post-graduate qualification in India, and my qualifications of

CIMA, CFA and MBA (from Booth School) for situations that I faced in my career. As for my family, hats off to them for moving away from the plush life in Jakarta and coming to Bombay with me. They learned a lot about the good life in Jakarta.

Returning to Bombay meant that we had to move away from all our close friends, with whom we had built strong relationships in the previous 13 years. But we took this too in our stride.

Key takeaways

In the life of every person, the mid-20s throw up several opportunities for taking bold steps. Seize these opportunities.

Relocating occasionally exposes you to varied experiences and cultures and improves your adaptability. As John Maxwell says, 'There is no growth in your comfort zone and there is no comfort in your growth zone.'

Adaptability is the key.

Knowledge, backed by formal learning and applied wisely, always helps you thrive.

Caring for parents, especially in the twilight years of their life, yields the ultimate satisfaction.

Please provide your views, comments, feedback and share what parts of this chapter resonates with you here

Link: https://srinivas.powervisionelectrical.co.in/
chapter-5-moving-away-from-the-rat-race/

Chapter 6

Developing the Right Mindset

We spend years in school and college learning various subjects and topics, many of which we hardly use in our life later. How many of us use calculus, trigonometry or Raoult's Law in daily life? There are many other such topics that we've left behind in school or college.

But unfortunately, the topic that every one of us needs to master to grow, succeed and live happily is not taught by most education systems across the world even today: developing the right mindset.

Traits of the growth mindset

Link 1: https://www.youtube.com/watch?v=b2HInbYxL58
Duration: 01:36 Mts.

Traits of strong growth mindset. Our ability to solve any problem is always bigger than the size of the problem, so let us develop a mindset not to overestimate the problem and underestimate our capabilities to solve them. We always should be having a perspective like the hair and the nails, always resilient and relentless, no matter what the situation is, they always keep growing. So we need to develop a mindset that

> will always be growing. We rarely say the trees are getting old, we only say the trees are growing. Similarly, as we move from one phase of life to another let us say that we are growing more wiser. Finally, let us have a mindset which is very strong. When our mindset is weak, we see situations as problems. When our mindset is balanced, we see situations as challenges. However, when our mindset is strong, we see situations as opportunities.

Like the word itself indicates, mindset is about setting your mind a certain way — *shaping it* a certain way. Which means having the right outlook, attitude and approach vis-à-vis life and its various aspects. This doesn't come to us overnight; it has to be imbibed from various sources around us and through introspection, and nurtured over the years. The earlier we start doing this, the better for us. Unfortunately, most of us begin to even grasp the fundamentals of this word only in our thirties or forties; some not even then. Remember this: even if you don't have a certain talent, skill, knowledge or type of experience, you can acquire it if you have the right mindset. In short, your mindset is the most important factor in deciding the quality of your life — your career, relationships, happiness, wealth, health and everything else.

I learned these lessons at various junctures of life, and they have stood me in great stead.

My first lessons in the growth mindset and in finding creative solutions to problems came from my dad, who, like I have said earlier, worked for Life Insurance Corporation of India (LIC). On most days, he used to recount to us children the challenges he faced in office, some of them quite knotty. He would tell us how he resolved them creatively, without creating agony or angst in his colleagues. We used to look forward to hearing these stories during dinner or afterwards. It was only years later that I realised that I was catching these vibes and lessons from him subconsciously. I started applying the lessons in various situations even in my childhood.

For instance, we were a family of six crammed into a tiny tenement in Bombay. I had difficulty in studying during regular hours — because my three siblings would also be studying in the same room at the same time!

So, after giving it some thought, I started studying late at night, when the others had gone to bed. This is how I finished my lessons and homework for years. So I didn't have any backlog; I also didn't have to cram my lessons just before an exam. And I used to somewhat compensate for my lack of nocturnal sleep with a nap in the afternoon, before my grandpa came home to teach me maths.

Thanks to my dad's strict regime, I could imbibe this culture. I managed to do reasonably well in my studies in school.

On respecting and managing time

Link 2: https://youtu.be/ieObiLHy4-o
Duration: 00:47 Mts.

> We will talk about handling and managing time. Enjoy and make use of every moment in life because time once passed will never come again. Akin to the river water once you touch it, it will never be possible to touch the same flow of stream again. That's why the old adage, time is money will prevail forever. The way we have respected time in the past, in terms of building relationships, in terms of upscaling and in terms of developing our competency is solely going to be deciding our fate in the immediate future.

Years later, I enrolled for the CFA course administered by ICFAI, an institute based in Hyderabad. Midway through this course, an occasion arose for me to move to Hong Kong; I got a better job there. Like I said earlier, this move would help me raise the money needed to join a particularly useful international course I had in mind (CIMA). But this move, from India to Hong Kong, could have created hassles in my continuing the CFA course. So what did I do? I spoke to the people at ICFAI and arranged for them to send my study materials to Hong Kong. I then arranged with the Indian embassy in Hong Kong to let me write the CFA exams on their premises in Hong Kong. And so, with a bit of creative thinking, I prevented a potentially major roadblock in my studies and career.

Another useful lesson I picked up in my childhood is to say 'no' when required. Trying to please everyone, or fitting into someone else's plans all the time, works to our disadvantage. My child's mind must have somehow realised this. And so, I used to emphatically say no to distractions such as family gatherings and outings. Even when the rest of my family went to the cinema, I would stay back at home if I had to study a lesson or work on a project. It's a matter of priorities, really. And priorities differ from person to person, and from juncture to juncture in life. The habit I inculcated in myself early on has remained with me until now; I focus on my priorities and say no to everything else.

Another element of the right mindset is gratitude. Closely related to this is the intent to make the most of what we have, rather than whining about what we don't. Though I knew this earlier, it was driven home to me powerfully by an incident in Hong Kong.

I was hired through a placement agency in South Bombay for this job in Hong Kong. It was normal practice to enter Hong Kong on a tourist visa, which would be replaced by a work visa later on. I was forewarned that I had to be carrying my passport at all times for as long as I was in Hong Kong on a tourist visa. And yet, one day, while travelling by metro train to my new place of residence, I was booked by the police for not carrying my passport. The silly thing happened to be with the immigration department, since my employment visa was being processed by them.

Thinking on my feet, I took the permission of the police officials to call up my office. I explained my precarious position to the staff. Thankfully, the receptionist promptly arrived at the police station, which was just about a kilometre from my office, to rescue me by producing my passport.

On invoking positivity

Link 3: https://youtu.be/c0lY0NMUeNY
Duration: 00:46 Mts.

> In this difficult world brought about by overwhelming responsibilities and overriding commitments, it's high time we start a new trend of invoking possible positivity at every opportunity. We could say 'Thanks' instead of 'Sorry. In case, if we are delayed we can say 'Thanks for Waiting' instead of 'Sorry I'm delayed'. This will help to improve the way you think about yourself and convey gratitude to the other person and avoid negativity.

This incident strengthened my belief that I was living on an extended lifeline — borrowed time, so to speak. From then on, I treated every hour of my stay in Hong Kong as a precious asset. During the day, I was mono-manically focused on work. And in the evening and night, I set up a disciplined schedule to study the academic courses I had signed up for. I was grateful for my job in that country, which let me earn much more than what I would have in India, and fund my higher professional studies. This, in turn, helped me lift my family from their tight financial circumstances.

The idea of thinking positively stems from the belief that our mind has got the ability to come up with solutions to any problem. All we need to do is keep focussing; a solution will soon become apparent. Also, we must make the most of every day. As and when I faced challenges later, I have always thought back to my situation in Hong Kong and drawn new strength and purpose from it.

On invoking the power of the mind

Link 4: https://youtu.be/Rs4s3GblcNE
Duration: 01:05 Mts.

> On invoking the power of mind: Each one of us are aware of 'The Power of Mind'. It can enslave us or it can empower us; it can plunge us into the depths of misery or it can rise us to the height of ecstasy. It is for us to keep strengthening it and using it wisely. That is why we keep hearing from seniors to be mindful. What are the benefits? Once we invoke the power of mind the right way, we will realize that contentment is the best form of wealth. Ensuring the company of wise person is the best attainment. Reflection is the paramount form of knowledge and quietude of the mind is the zenith of happiness.

Arrogance sets in under two circumstances, mainly. One, when you are wrong and can't face it. And two, when you are right and others can't face it. I've found that it's best to stay away from arrogance and embrace humility. In fact, more and more experts consider humility as a hallmark of true leadership. The best leaders in the world in any arena are approachable, kind and empathetic. This comes from their humility. Arrogance scars, while humility generates love and goodwill.

On being humble

Link 5: https://youtu.be/Dwl4uWJbEMA
Duration: 00:45 Mts.

> On being humble: There are two circumstances, when we try to set in arrogance, especially, when placed in a position of power. One is when you are wrong and you can't face it. The other situation is, when you are right and others can't face it. Let us try to side step the situation by attempting to be humble, so that we can avoid leaving a scar on the other person or the people around us.

My dad was humble and large-hearted. I told you how, when he had settled down well in LIC in Bombay, he brought his siblings from their village to Bombay and made them live with him, so they could have a better life. He kept them with him until each one of them found their feet in their respective careers.

I have tried to carry forward this legacy of my father. For instance, in Hong Kong, I had the opportunity to help a distant relative of mine. He was stranded in Hong Kong when his rogue employer absconded with money, after cheating some banks by forging documents. I went against my flat mate's wish to give unconditional shelter to this relative. Incidentally, he became a very close friend thereafter; he continues to be one even today, although we are distanced by continents.

Generosity breeds generosity. Life is a cycle; one never knows who will be extending their wings to rescue you when you are in dire need one day.

The incident I mentioned just now occurred in the year 1995. Fast-forward by 21 years. In 2016, my son Krishnan had to travel alone to Toronto for his graduate studies. Now, the same relative cum friend I had helped in Hong Kong came to our rescue. He agreed to be Krishnan's legal guardian in Canada. He extended all possible support to Krishnan to ensure his comfortable stay in Toronto from 2016 to 2020. And, when Covid-19 hit the world like a typhoon in March 2020 and there was a ban on international flights, this person was kind enough to shelter Krishnan in his house until he could return to India under the Vande Bharat mission announced by the Indian government.

On being connected with charismatic people

Link 6: https://youtu.be/H4tdUp-SIt8
Duration: 00:33 Mts.

> Cheerful and charismatic people endowed with abundant grace are hard to find by. They are like pleasant sunlight on a cool morning in a hill station. They shine in each corner of your heart, give lot of inspiration and help you to create ray of hope. Can you find one nearby.

You need to believe in yourself and be the leader of your life. What we achieve internally (in our spirit and mind) will be reflected in our outer reality.

Leadership Guru Robin Sharma has said, 'The way we do little things in life is the way we will do everything in life.'

Those little things in life

Link 7: https://youtu.be/sBwqljgt5Xs
Duration: 00:52 Mts.

> Those little things in life: Little hugs can dry big tears, little memory can last forever, little bit of appreciation can encourage many. Little bits of thought can avoid undesirable steps. It is those little things that can bring big happiness and make an impact in our life. Before starting any activity positively, appreciate yourself and you will see a big change in your performance. If you develop the habit of that little recognition for yourself and encouragement, what little things are you going to start today?

For instance, if you are successful on the personal front, you will likely be successful on the professional front also. We have to handle variables in any walk of life, whether we are in our hometown or elsewhere. Once you have got used to the habit of handling changes and challenges in India and abroad, you will be able to find solutions to any variable you come across anywhere.

We need a balance between mindset, healthset, heartset and soulset, as explained by Robin Sharma in his book *The 5 AM Club*. I realised that I had been practising some of these concepts well before he wrote about them.

Once we develop the right mindset and the culture to think appropriately in any situation, we start evolving solutions to the challenges we face in life.

On handling worries in life

Link 8: https://youtu.be/rNE7tmIU-Ew
Duration: 00:42 Mts.

> Worries in life are not due to circumstances prevailing but born out of our mental weakness. How do we get rid of these worries? Accept changes, expect changes and learn to enjoy changes in all walks of life. Neurons that wire together fire together. So, train yourself to wire your brain to think positive in all conditions.

The proper healthset, born out of fitness or exercise, will directly help in creating the right mindset in you. I'd go as far as to say that it is a pre-condition for the right mindset. Take my father, for instance. As I indicated before, my father used to treat his morning walk as a ritual. He wouldn't sacrifice it for anything. The image of my father returning from his walk every morning is stuck in my mind. It was because of him that I imbibed the practice of strengthening my healthset in my childhood itself. Other than playing cricket almost every day, I made exercise a daily ritual. Over time, I noticed that this habit — my healthset — helped me develop the right mindset. And, since I have retained this habit through all these years, I continue to reap its benefits.

I am convinced that this link between health and the mind, and seeing dad lead a reasonably successful life, helped me take a number of right decisions for my personal and professional advancement.

Another crucial aspect of success is insane focus. This is related to something I said earlier: identifying our priorities and saying no to everything else. This clears our mind of distractions and allows us to focus on what is truly important to us — what we *really, really* want. Every now and then, ask yourself what you really, really want. And then focus your efforts on the answer you get, clearing your life of distractions.

On saying yes and no

Link 9: https://youtu.be/TesqlJutfxE
Duration: 00:46 Mts.

> We will talk about Risk and Regret, 'Yes' and 'No' are two short words which actually require a deep thought and a long pause to avoid any risks. Most of the things that we miss in life are because of saying 'No' too early or 'Yes' too late especially on bold steps in life. Deliberation and consultation with experienced seniors will likely avoid this risk and regret.

This is what I did in Indonesia for almost 13 years. My love for cricket and my ambition to play the game at the highest level made me shun a lot of other things that are common in the life of the regular person, especially the expat (outings, movies, parties, etc.). I practised at the nets regularly, and was selected for playing in my club's team, then the Jakarta regional team and finally, in the years 2005 and 2007, in the Indonesia national team. All this was not easy. But thinking methodically and putting my priorities ahead of everything else played a big part. And of course, I was ably backed by my spouse. (More on the qualities of my spouse later in this book.)

The same thing happened when we planned to return to India in 2010. My first two attempts to return to India were abortive. The opportunities available in the Bombay office of Crown Worldwide did not work out. So I had to stay back in Jakarta for a few more years. But I did not get upset.

Instead, I started working on moving from my functional role to a general role by training myself and working with my boss to see what I could learn and do beyond my function. And these changes prepared me mentally to take up a much bigger role in India when I finally snagged a transfer in 2010. I could work with my wife to take the bold call of returning to India. This was in the wake of the Lehman Brothers collapse, which had led to a global financial meltdown. A number of my well-wishers and friends advised us not to go to India. But I was clear in my thinking: we were going there to take care of our aged and unwell parents; this was paramount to us at that time. And we did return to Bombay and establish ourselves rather well there.

Sometimes, early success might elude you (like my initial attempts to get transferred to Bombay). But take the failures in your stride and, learning from those failures, prepare yourself for a better tomorrow. Biding your time often helps.

There is always a way to work through your options instead of getting frustrated. In continuation of my earlier tale, when I came to India in 2010, I found that almost everything was falling apart in the India operations of Crown. But I took this as a blessing in disguise because I could work through several options before arriving at a formula that would help my company and I succeed in India, a tough market. It been 13 years since then. I've managed to transform India into one of the best-performing operations for Crown globally. The way I look at it, my initial failures (to come to India in 2002 and 2006) helped me sit down and plan, think harder about how to hone my abilities, and learn how to build and run a team well. And, when I finally got the transfer to Bombay in 2010, to don a crucial role, I was ready for it in every sense! No wonder things worked out exceedingly well for me from then on.

On tough times

Link 10: https://www.youtube.com/watch?v=CzWCTRyMb3w
Duration: 00:30 Mts.

> Each one of us go through tough times. Tough times are like physical exercises, we may not like it when we are doing it. Later we are sure to emerge stronger. Similarly, the stress hormones released after our tough times will help us grow.

I have been with Crown Worldwide for 25 years. But even today, I treat every day as my first day at work and do not take my position for granted. Nor do I bask in the glory of my past. And I encourage all my team mates to adopt this approach too.

Focus and a disciplined approach are critical if we are trying to crack a problem we have not encountered before. Though people encounter new problems in any industry, this is especially common in the industry in which I work. You need to evolve a solution creatively instead of just applying a straight-jacketed formula that may have worked before. Unconventional creative thinking is increasingly becoming the norm in every field, given the VUCA (vulnerable, uncertain, complex and ambiguous) times we are in.

Meditation is another habit that has helped me immensely. The form of meditation I learned at home is the chanting of certain mantras after I started wearing the sacred thread. It is a custom for boys in Brahmin families in India to be initiated into wearing the janeu or poonool (the sacred thread), and chanting these mantras every day.

On a basic level, a mantra is believed to contain immensely divine potency. When narrated in the stipulated manner, it releases divine sound and energy. The energy fabric itself has five elements: light, heat, magnetism, electricity and sound. The efficacy of any mantra taught under proper conditions by qualified priests after our sacred thread ceremony involves certain preliminary rituals and invocations using water, meditation and prayers. And the efficacy is enhanced when one performs the rituals and chants with a pure heart in the specified tone, with clarity, fully knowing their meaning. There's a strong belief that chanting these mantras contributes to one's wellbeing and that of the others in the family. It is believed that the earlier in our youth we get used to narrating and memorising these, and the longer and better we chant them, the better we internalise them. Mind you, it is neither easy nor popular. But it is believed to be immensely beneficial. At least, I feel I have benefited from this practice.

Actually, any form of prayer is meditation. We must take a cue from our brothers from the Islamic countries. In Indonesia for instance, I was amazed to see the discipline with which Indonesian Muslims used to pray 5 times a day. During the month of Ramadan, most of them followed the rigorous routine of waking up early in the morning, finishing their meal and then not eating anything for as long as 11 to 12 hours. And yet, they'd continue to pray 5 times a day and carry on with their daily activities!

So meditation is not unusual or very difficult. All it needs is a willing mind.

On willpower

Link 11: https://youtu.be/opSv5N3lsKQ
Duration: 01:01 Mts.

> On will power: James Flynn, the Kiwi Psychologist coined a term called 'Capitalization IQ'. The difference between successful people and others is neither the lack of strength nor the lack of knowledge. But a sheer lack in exercising ones will power. Will Power is like a body muscle the more you exercise the better you get at it. Success solely lies around consistently in this fundamental. Capitalization is not your talent, but the ability to exercise your potential that you are born with by using your 'Will Power'. Have you exercised your capitalization IQ through 'Will Power'?

I had the opportunity to get trained under an Indian yogi, a spiritual master. This helped me have a calm mind, and reduce my stress, anxiety and depression. The routines I leaned from him have energised my body, improved my health, and reduced my weight. And empowered me to handle many unpleasant situations at work.

Consistently following the spiritual steps on an empty stomach helped me benefit personally and professionally. I credit my meditative practices with helping me set up a well-balanced team and grow the Crown business in India.

So yes, meditation has immense benefits, provided one is ready to discipline oneself and follow certain practices on a daily basis. You start deriving solutions to challenges. But remember: what you do daily matters more than what you do once in a while. It's not easy, and you need to go through a process. But it can be done.

A few final thoughts.

Our ability to solve any problem is always bigger than the size of the problem. We must not overestimate the problem and underestimate our ability to solve it.

Be the leader of your life. Lead yourself to where you want to be. Breathe life back into your ambitions.

Enjoy and make use of every moment of life. Time, once passed, can never be touched again.

Develop a strong mind. Worries are born out of mental weakness.

Key takeaways

Courage does not always roar. Sometimes courage is the quiet voice that says at the end of the day, 'I will try again tomorrow to succeed.'

Your calm mind is the ultimate weapon against your challenge, so relax! – Thought leader Bryant McGill

You can't achieve beyond your level of development. You don't achieve goals. You grow into them. – American entrepreneur Jim Rohn

Please provide your views, comments, feedback and share what parts of this chapter resonates with you here

Link: https://srinivas.powervisionelectrical.co.in/chapter-6-developing-the-right-mindset/

Chapter 7

Building Strong Relationships

Talent and looks are God-given; be thankful.
Fame and money are created with a lot of effort, given the right conditions; be grateful.
Attitude and ego are self-created; be extremely careful.

On relationships

Link 1: https://youtu.be/MrZeCQPJquw
Duration: 00:38 Mts.

> The purpose of relationship in life with anyone, especially the closed one is not who may be with you completely, but who may be there to understand your incompleteness completely. In other words, quality matters more than quantity and depth matters more than duration.

While hard work, sacrifice, upskilling myself and a bit of luck have had a hand in my growth and success in different roles, I must acknowledge another big factor also: my relationships.

Early on, I realised that the quality of the relationships I enjoy with people has a huge impact on how I live. And over the years, this realisation has only been validated and deepened, leaving me a much better person who enjoys a more rounded and fulfilling life with each passing day.

When we talk about relationships, we usually think of ourselves vis-à-vis others. But what about our relationship with ourselves? I think this is the first aspect one has to look at when talking about forging strong, healthy relationships. Before we start examining our relationships with others or assessing in what ways they have to be improved, we must assess our relationship with our own selves. *What is my relationship with myself?*

This may sound a bit strange, even weird. But it's true, and vital.

From time to time, I mull over whether I respect myself without being a megalomaniac. Whether I love myself without getting narcissistic. Whether I look at myself with compassion and generosity. Whether I empathise with myself. Why? Because, only when I do all this can I extend the same treatment to others and build healthy, lasting relationships with them.

In every relationship, we need to listen to the other person with ears of tolerance. We need to develop the habit of seeing them and their actions with eyes of compassion. We need to learn to speak the language of empathy and care. Earning a relationship is a reward for our trust, maintaining it is the result of our sacrifice, and strengthening it is a result of our care.

A relationship is not a business, where we give only when we get something in return. It is a beautiful state of being, in which we give everything even if we don't *get* anything. Relationships are built not by forcing others to understand you, but by giving them the confidence that you will never misunderstand them unless there are consistent fault lines.

Based on my personal, professional, social and spiritual experiences over the past three and half decades, I can share with you a few principles I have applied in forging relationships with my colleagues and others. These people are of different nationalities and belong to different walks of life.

In general, when you are with a group of people, mind your behaviour. And to nurture a relationship with someone who has become a close acquaintance, mind your tongue. I have come across various types of people, but have never regretted trying to forge a relationship with them — even if only distant ones. If a relationship is good, it generates pleasant memories. And if it is not, it serves as an experience. This is applicable to anyone. Irrespective of the nature of a relationship, we need to enjoy the path of life. Remember, what goes around comes around. So always try to keep your circle positive by speaking good words, thinking good thoughts and doing good deeds.

Another simple yet extremely potent credo that has worked for me is to not expect too much from anyone. It is always better to get surprised (even delighted) than to be disappointed by someone. No matter how well you behave with people, most of them will like you (or not) according to their moods and needs. So stay as simple as you can and keep your expectations at ground level, though this is extremely difficult to do.

Even in my family, we have always applied this credo. I'm referring to my children, my wife Jayashree and myself. The silken bonds of love and respect keep us together. Our family life is uncomplicated, free and happy, with each person having the space to do their own thing.

While I could fill pages with the principles of building strong relationships, it would be worth penning down a few things I learned from a special set of friends when I was in Hong Kong for three years.

Year 1995

Year 2023

These folks hailed from Madras (now called Chennai). I first met them in May 1994. And, even after nearly three decades, we are in touch regularly, each of us sharing our progress, challenges, joys and sorrows with the others. Incidentally, all of them continue to live in Hong Kong with their families even today. They have enjoyed life and continue to do so, not because only good things have come their way but because *they find the good in everything that came their way.* They firmly believe that life doesn't introduce you to only the people you want to meet. It brings you in contact with people of all kinds. It is up to you to deal with them well and make the most out of your acquaintance with them.

Based on this belief system, I learned that some people come to help us and some come to hurt us, whereas some meet us and leave us after just a few interactions. And then there are those who stay with us for a long time, continuing to love us.

These friends of mine also believe that interacting with different sets of people gradually strengthens us into the persons we are meant to become for a stronger tomorrow. So, instead of harping on finding only 'good' people, they have always had the habit of searching for the good in whoever they came across, ignoring the bad in them. Being with them for three years opened my eyes to several wonderful, intricate and crucial aspects of relationships.

No one is perfect. So it is inevitable that most if not all relationships will run into a rough patch, now and then. Now, how do we handle these patches?

Well, a relationship is similar to a dictionary. It provides meaning and explanation to only those who refer to it regularly and decipher it properly. When you're angry with friends, mind your temper — to preserve the relationship capital. To build a strong relationship, we don't always have to agree with one another. But it is important that we learn to respect each other. Open and clear communication is a lifeline for any relationship to continue and even thrive. When you stop communicating, you lose all valuable relationships. If you have a problem with someone but want to continue the relationship, you have to talk to them. If you experience problems with too many people, you must talk to yourself!

In any relationship, a discussion is an exchange of thoughts and knowledge. Inculcate and promote the habit of discussing things. But an argument is an exchange of ego and ignorance. Avoid it at all costs. If you want to maintain a steadfast relationship with someone, believe in only what you know about them, not what you've heard about them. Hold no grudges, and learn to practise forgiveness. This is the key to keeping peace in every relationship.

Friendship and love can be medicines for any pain in life. But we have to be careful not to misuse them. Otherwise, they may end up scarring us for life.

I have learned that relationships have a potentially messy side too. They can be misused. They can end up hurting us if we don't nurture them well. Which is why I said earlier that, first of all, we need to get rid of our expectations from people. When we do that, we remove their power to hurt our feelings. Our joy and sorrow depend on where our mind is focussed. If we keep thinking of false, fake or unwanted situations most of the time, and if we rake these up frequently in conversations with our relatives, friends, colleagues or others, we cause hurt and pain. We then qualify to be branded as a problem child — a person creating problems in any relationship.

So train your mind to pick pleasant topics in any conversation. Relationships are not where you find happiness. Relationships are where you *share* happiness. It is a two-way process; listening with an open mind is a vital part of it.

For more than three decades, I have been friends with someone called Ravi, who I first met at an informal gathering of college mates in Bombay. We became fast friends after the first few interactions and, though life has taken us down widely different paths over the years, we have stayed close to each other all along. It is worth highlighting a few things we have practiced for the last three and a half decades.

We have realised that life is a combination of adjustments and compromises. We notice good things in each other as quickly as we notice mistakes. We are frank enough to identify flaws and limitations in each other whenever we spot them. But on each of those points, we have only corrected and forgiven each other, never held a grudge. We have only offered constructive criticism. And we have always appreciated what's good in each other. As a result, we've established a strong bond. And even today, we consult each other frequently on areas where hopes have to be converted into aspirations and aspirations into results. This has worked wonders for both of us, personally and professionally, in all these years. We could not stay in close touch for a few years in between, due to unavoidable circumstances (we were busy settling down in our respective professional fields). But even this separation only strengthened our attachment.

On maintaining relationships

Link 2: https://youtu.be/QIwnIn-To-k
Duration: 00:59 Mts.

> Relationship: Well, relationship should be maintained with friends', relatives and acquaintances reasonably, always in great terms. Especially as we move from one facet of life to another; as we grow from a young person to adulthood to old age. We can actually link relationship to two zeros, when you add two zeros; the result is the same. When you subtract one zero from the other, the result is the same. But when we try to divide it; it becomes impossible to continue. So let us try to maintain the relationship, irrespective of the status or hierarchy we reach in our life.

Life will always be full of challenges. As we brace for an uncertain tomorrow, it is advisable to reflect on things that have helped us reach where we are today, especially if we've grown quite consistently in the past. Look backwards with satisfaction and move forward with confidence. Always count your blessings, rather than the pitfalls, losses and deficiencies.

You are a human being. Life is a circle of happiness and sadness, good times and hard times. Reflect on these oscillating facts of life. If you're going through hard times, have faith that good times are around the corner. The dark night will end and the sun will rise. The way we start the day sets up the day. Look at the sky, treating every day as a blessing. And admire the freshness of the morning. Count your little blessings and successes — and you may be surprised to find several of them, once you start counting — every day. All this will certainly cool your senses if you do it consistently.

Viewing problems as situations

Link 3: https://youtu.be/R_4cOlsg_1k
Duration: 01:00 Mts.

> We will look at viewing problems as situations. As we pass through different phases of growth cycle until retirement or even until death, we come across life as having full of problems. Problems are not Permanent. Life has to be taken in its stride as we go through. As we keep facing problems, we need to see it as situations and find a way to handle it, based on the circumstances and keep moving on. Then these problems can be seen as challenges and/or situations. And as we keep adept at solving these situations, we can drive through different phases of life. That's what life is and let us enjoy it.

As Robin Sharma says in his book *The 5 AM club*, 'A day is nothing but the miniature of our entire life.' If we are consistent in taking up all personal and professional activities on a positive note, magic begins to happen over a period. This was the secret that helped me transition from my role in Indonesia (as a functional expert) to a new one in India (Country Head).

Faith is a short word, but it has deep implications. Having faith and hope is what takes one to the realm of excellence. Others around you catch these vibes subconsciously when you share your turnaround stories with them. And, when you hear their stories of growth, you too will be inspired by them!

Though it has now been a dozen years since I left Indonesia to come to India, I continue to maintain strong relationships with many of my friends there, in my work, sports and social circles. Of course, social media has had a hand in keeping us close, but the bedrock of these relationships is not that. It is our investment of time and effort from the years 1997 to 2010, when I lived there with my family. My colleagues, fellow professional cricketers, friends and I inculcated a feel-good culture through every gentle touch or interaction of ours. We gave each other hugs and handshakes where it mattered. We always saw good in every face. We always heard good in every word. We treated every interaction as a sheer blessing. We made sure to demonstrate genuine love and compassion as necessities, not luxuries. If it hadn't been for this foundation of mutual affection, respect and honesty, and the small gestures that reflected these sentiments, these relationships would most probably have dissipated after a short while.

It is said that time decides who you meet in life, the heart decides who you want in life, and your behaviour decides who will stay in your life.

It is not difficult to attempt to start a relationship, in friendship or in love. No relationship is a waste of time. If it didn't bring you what you wanted, it would have at least taught you what you didn't want. We attract people by the qualities we display. But forging a close connection and retaining people in our lives can only happen because of qualities you possess and which you nurture over a long period of time. Forging a close connection begins to happen when relationships are deepened; not by talking big but by understanding small feelings.

Also, 'sorry' works when mistakes are made, but not when trust is broken. So in life, make mistakes, but never break someone's trust — as forgiving is easy, but forgetting and trusting again is sometimes impossible.

The ultimate test is on the shore of life. All good relationships are like waves. They come and go, but some touch you in such a way that the feeling of closeness remains forever. Only then can you conclude that you have forged a strong connection with the people in question.

Sacrifice is always greater than love. Character is always greater than beauty. And humanity is always greater than wealth. And through the qualities of sacrifice, character and humanity, we can forge and maintain good relationships.

A final word of caution. I have learned to never take any relationship for granted but to be vigilant always. In the process, be kind but never allow myself to be taken for granted or abused. 'Trust, but don't be deceived' is a dictum that has served me very well. Also, be content in a relationship, but never stop improving yourself to improve the relationship. Irrespective of the strength or duration of a relationship, never allow your kindness to be treated as your weakness. In this respect, you should have the wisdom to walk away when you absolutely have to. Being able to walk away is courage, and doing so with your head held high is dignity.

Remember this always.

On letting someone go

Link 4: https://youtu.be/8irFZajGZP4
Duration: 00:41 Mts.

> Peace of Mind is the most valuable asset for every one of us especially in this stressful world. That said, when some people walk away from your life you should let them go. Your fortune is never tied to their presence. That does not mean they are bad people, it is just that their

chapter in your book is over. They might come back to you in the form of annexures later in life. Hard pill to swallow, but essential for our Peace of Mind.

Key takeaways

You don't meet people by accident. There's always a reason — a blessing or a lesson.

Let the limitations of other people not limit you. And 'someone's wrong' isn't an excuse for *you* to be wrong. Wrong as a response to wrong is not the right way.

Never take any relationship for granted; similarly, never let anyone take you for granted.

Work on improving yourself and on improving your relationships.

I can do things you cannot, you can do things I cannot. Together we can do great things.

Please provide your views, comments, feedback and share what parts of this chapter resonates with you here

Link: https://srinivas.powervisionelectrical.co.in/chapter-7-building-strong-relationships/

Chapter 8

The Principles of Success

Only those who have seen you struggle will know the true worth of your success. For the others, you are just 'fortunate'.

Yes and no are two short words that require deep thought and a long pause. Most of the things we miss in life are because we say no too early or yes too late.

On saying yes and no

Link 1: https://youtu.be/TesqlJutfxE
Duration: 00:48 Mts.

> Risk and Regret: 'Yes' and 'No' are two short words which actually require a deep thought and a long pause to avoid any risks. Most of the things that we miss in life are because of saying 'No' too early or 'Yes' too late especially on bold steps. In life, deliberation and consultation with experienced seniors will likely avoid this risk and regret.

Take bold steps in life. That's when you'll do something big and meaningful and make a mark. This requires deep thought and long pauses. Pause your frenetic activity and think. This, along with consulting experienced seniors, will help you avoid or mitigate risks.

Principles of success

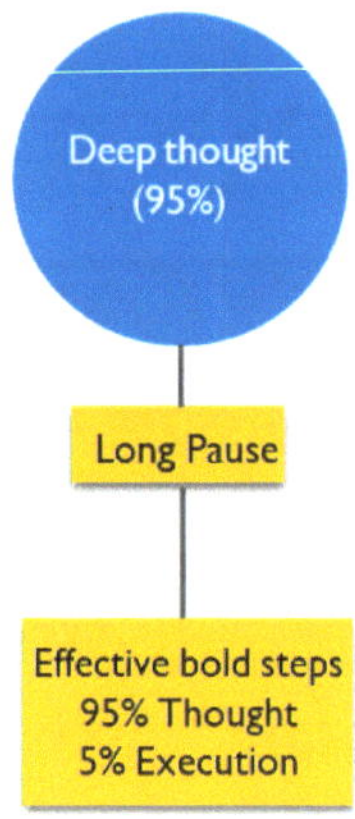

Always be positive

Creativity is 95% thought-process and 5% execution. Creativity is the gap between the world of reality and the world of imagination (which is boundless). Imagination is a powerful tool that can be used to create and explore new possibilities. Creativity can be used to solve complex problems and arrive at innovative solutions to difficult challenges. This is what is going to fetch a premium for you if you are looking to make it big in life.

Amarnath yatra

Link 2: https://www.youtube.com/watch?v=cZTnGfU78Bo

Duration: 04:52 Mts.

Lord Jagannath's rath yatra

Link 3: https://www.youtube.com/watch?v=qREtDNzBcRs
Duration: 04:39 Mts.

The traditional steps decked with decoration and lighting, aligned to make an impact is called the 'Golu' in Tamil. I'm sure you're enjoying it. What makes this different, this year from what we had until last year; is the surface area used to place these meticulously collected dolls over the last few years. The idea is to maximize the space by redesigning those dimensions of the steps to accommodate more Dolls, yet display a marvellous arrangement.

What is the theme all about 'Yatra'; this is the replica of Lord Jagannath puri's famous 'Rath Yatra'. It is easier to procure the items. But not show to arrange the Lord's journey in an orderly fashion meant to be mesmerizing to one's eyes. Here comes the Creator, inherently gifted and intimidatingly creative. This work is done by a qualified professional, who unconditionally gave up her career for the sake of family. But then it is said, true gold always glitters no matter where you are. Here is the person in charge, no title, no position, no importance in the society, but a true artist. Guess who is it. Traditionally we have had this practice of keeping Golu in our house since 1970s till the year 1990 in our Jeevan Kala residence in Mumbai in India. Jayashree came to our house in 1998 after we got married, of course an arranged one. This practice of keeping Golu during Navratri started in Jakarta, Indonesia in the year 2004. Two years after our little princess Lakshita's entry into this world. Pleasantly this culture spread to other house from the following year with wealthy families competing to outdo one another, thus forming a revolution of keeping Golu every year. Jayashree has followed this tradition even after her return from Jakarta for family reasons since the

> year 2011, without using the size of the house which was limited or lack of support as a constraint. This all goes to show that what one needs is a pure determination of the mind and will of the heart with openness to experiment. Do come to our house. If you are located away; your valuable feedback on a scale of 1 to 10 will do a world of good. To decide how we can improvise this Feast to one's eyes. Going forward to know more about the Advent of the temple you are most welcome to our house. Thanks for watching. May goddess Durga and Lord Jagannath continue to bless you.

These two links will take you to videos showing the miniatures of the Amarnath yatra and the chariot festival of Lord Jagannath, which takes place in Puri. My wife Jayashree made these replicas. Both these places are spread over vast areas. For example, the route of the Amarnath yatra is spread over several kilometres in Kashmir, whereas the chariot festival of Lord Jagannath takes place over several acres in the town of Puri in Odisha.

The replicas you see in the videos have been prepared with passion. It is the personal expression of the artiste, and is an example of her creativity. Jayashree prepared these in a record time of one month in a physical space that is less than 50 square feet. This is an excellent example of creativity in the face of constraints (in this case, space). The feedback to these videos on YouTube says it all. Jayashree spent 95% of the time *thinking* about how to recreate these massive locations in miniature form and just 5% of the time executing her thoughts.

When you are in the company of a highly imaginative life partner, any challenge presents solutions instead of seeming like a problem. Why? Because every person is the average of the few people they spend most of their time with. So the creative energy of these few people rubs off on you, and you are able to spot solutions easier than otherwise.

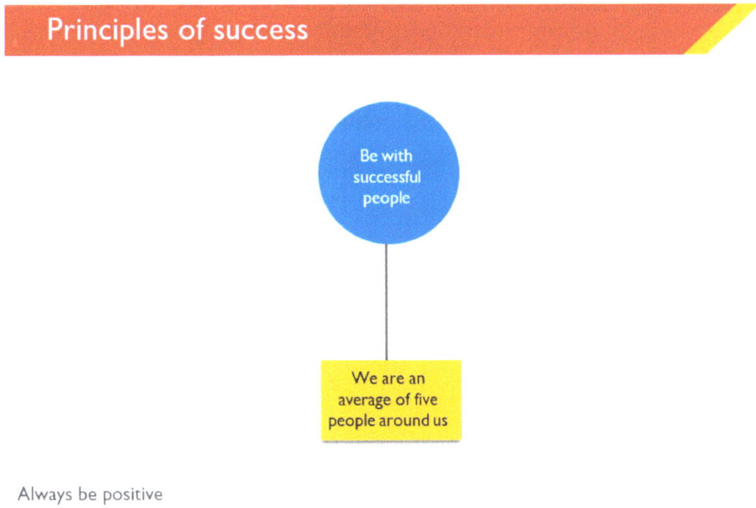

It is said that success is 5% inspiration and 95% perspiration. It is relatively easy to desire or visualise a concept and get inspired. What is needed is the tenacity and the ability to execute it with limited resources like money, time and space. This calls for a deadly combination of focus, talent, energy, will power, discipline and determination.

Be deliberate in your practice. This involves deeply focussing on a particular skill or activity. But before we delve deeper into deliberate practice, we must talk about mindfulness.

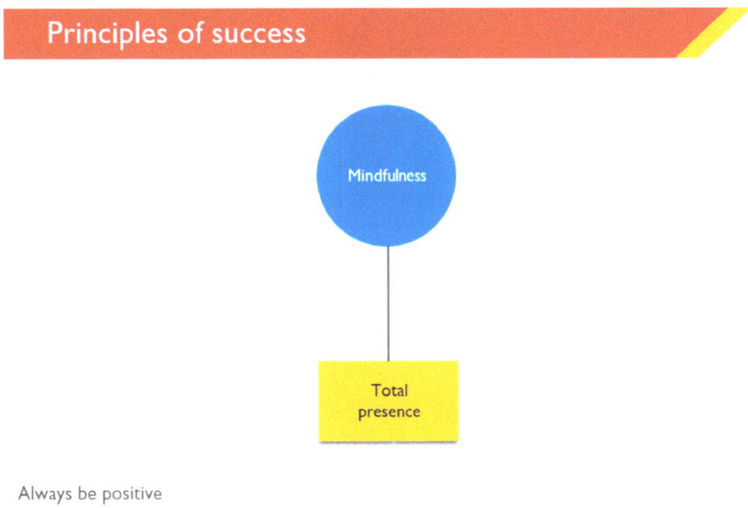

The mind is simply a wilful toddler. Mindfulness is the practice of gently focussing one's awareness on the present moment, over and over again. This has gained significance in this world of distraction and information overload. By practising mindfulness all the time with determination, discipline, patience and compassion for oneself, we can teach the mind to be still. It means that there is no intellectual filter between you and what you're experiencing. This experience is what is known as true presence.

Jayashree could not have made those miniatures I mentioned earlier without being totally present in the moment. In other words, without being mindful of what she was doing. She has been recreating different places of worship located in India, year after year, since 2004, during the Indian festival of Navratri. And she has been getting better and better over the years. In the process, she has never shied away from leveraging her ecosystem, seeking suggestions from experts in miniatures and referring to credible online resources.

Principles of success

Always be positive

Now we come to deliberate practice. There are myths and misconceptions surrounding deliberate practice in the context of learning and mastering something. It is confused with mere repetition, or mindlessly going through the motions.

What is deliberate practice?

Link 4: https://www.youtube.com/watch?v=h4JbjT09n8s
Duration: 02:05 Mts.

Deliberate Practice: In this pandemic, a lot of people have lost their jobs and everybody is looking forward to starting their own consultancy or a particular field. In this aspect or in this situation the concept of Deliberate Practice needs to be understood in the right earnest. Deliberate Practice involves focusing on a particular skill, it may be in sports or literature or any discipline. Ensuring that we measure the progress preferably under an instructor with feedback, which is informative on the progress being made. Like how the media distorts lots of facts there is a tendency by lots of management gurus and leadership coaches to confuse the Deliberate Practice with the 10,000 hour rule. The 10,000 hour rule was something which was study conducted by an expert on Deliberate Practice Mr. Erick Anderson. When he studied the musicians especially, the violinist in a particular school and concluded that on an average they took 10,000 hours of practice to become masters. However, that didn't mean that deliberate practice requires 10,000 hours of practice. This world with limited time and lot of stresses, one needs to be vary of ensuring that one gets down to the facts and not to confuse Deliberate Practice, which require focus and attention to realise your dreams on a particular area, instead of merely repeating it for 10,000 hours.

You may have heard of the 10,000-hour rule popularised by high profile authors in recent years. Many people have misunderstood this rule, thinking that it takes 10,000 hours of practice to gain mastery in any field.

But, K Anders Ericsson, an authority on deliberate practice, has busted this misconception through a study.

His study didn't find that it takes 10,000 hours — i.e., a specific number of hours — of practice for someone to master a field. It found that it takes massive amounts of *deliberate practice* to become very good in any field, with or without natural advantages. I hope you can spot the subtle difference between the two.

Principles of success

Always be positive

Dreams, desire, decision, deliberation, determination, drive and daily habits are the key Ds needed to develop our lives. In Ericsson's words, there is no reason to not follow your dream. Deliberate practice can open the door to a world of possibilities that you may have been convinced were out of reach.

No tact or effort is needed to dream big and achieve 'impossible' things. There is no limit to our desire. Desire decides our priorities. Priorities shape our choices. And choices determine our actions. But it is our bold decision to act that moves us towards our dream.

Any action we take as a consequence of our thoughtful decisions takes us a step closer to our dreams. Deliberation with experts and experienced people who seem to have gained wisdom gives us the much-needed confidence to pursue our dreams.

The difference between impossible and possible lies in one's dogged determination, developed over a period of time. Backed by all the sequential steps narrated here, instead of being pushed back by our problems, we should be led by our dreams.

Avoid the myth of linking happiness with time

Link 5: https://www.youtube.com/watch?v=ZJXlbzt7MhQ
Duration: 01:26 Mts.

The myth of linking time with happiness. This is a story I read, not sure if it is fictional or fact but worth sharing. In a large gathering that was addressed by a priest, one of the members in the audience asked him what was the happiest time in your life. The priest paused for a while and then asked him, 'what is your happiest time?' why do you tie happiness with time. What happens is, when time changes sometimes we have good time and sometimes we have bad time. However, linking time with happiness makes you search for happiness during bad times. If we accept life the way it comes, we will be happy all the time. The main search for happiness is the cause of unhappiness. Let's just learn to enjoy every moment in life; learn to realize that happiness has very little to do with time.

Principles of success

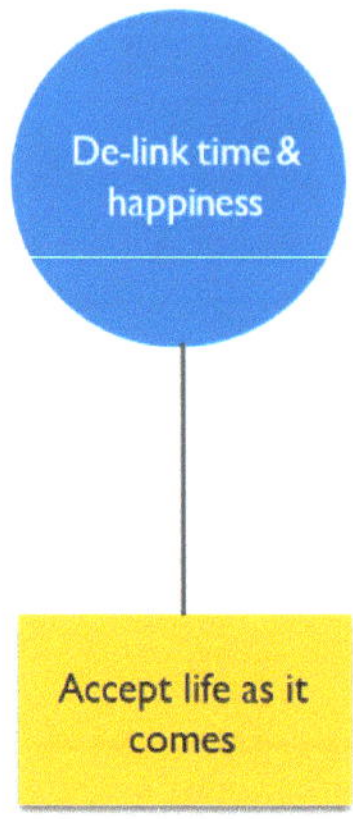

Always be positive

Do not link time with happiness. Doing this makes you search for happiness even in bad times. It's better to accept life as it comes. Then we will be happy all the time. Let us learn to enjoy every moment in life. Realise that happiness has little to do with time.

Life becomes much more meaningful when you realise that you'll never get the same moment and conditions twice. The drive comes by default. Thereby, self-discipline in the form of daily habits becomes the biggest investment for success in life.

For example, my decision to enroll myself in the Executive MBA program at Chicago Booth School of Business was initially a dream. But I made it a priority. I decided to join the program after consulting my bosses and peers who had already completed their MBA. And once I was in, it took dogged determination — putting in the effort over several tiring months — to convert my dream into reality.

Principles of success

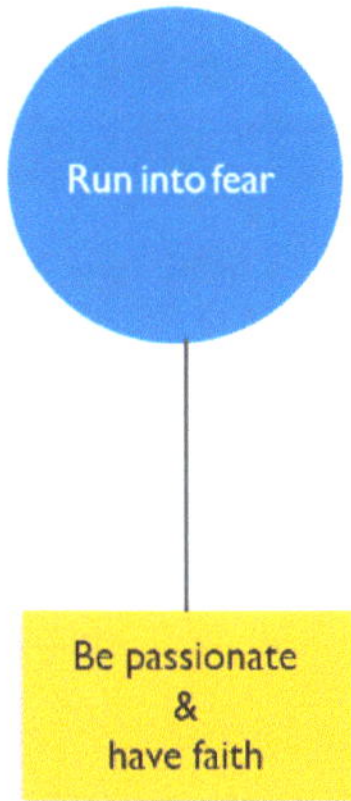

Always be positive

During a crisis, the greatest handicap is fear. But the beautiful thing about fear is that, when we run towards it, it runs away from us. Sometimes we think all the doors are closed in our life. But these closed doors may not be locked. Some of them will open in response to our bold knock and a nudge.

Take the time when, like I said earlier, in the wake of the Asian financial crisis in 1997, I persuaded my company's Country Head in Indonesia to bill customers in dollars. The Indonesian Rupiah was nosediving at the rate of 5% to 10%every week. Billing customers in dollars helped us signal value in the marketplace. Other companies in our industry started doing the same thing and earning an execution premium. So we became trendsetters in the industry. All because we went against the grain and knocked boldly on the door of that opportunity, a door that looked closed. Every crisis creates an opportunity, and it is for us to identify and exploit the same.

Our strength and acumen grow when we dare. Our connect with our teammates grows when we treat them fairly. Respect and relationships grow when we care for people genuinely. Knowledge and connect grow when we are willing to share unconditionally.

As far as forging connections is concerned, who can forget the Covid-19 pandemic? It taught us priceless lessons and opened our eyes to several fundamental realities of life and the human condition.

In our company, we continued our frequent communication with our team members, establishing a stronger connection with them. We gave them the confidence that we were there with them, and that the pandemic would not affect their jobs or livelihood, no matter how long it lasted. Also, during the Covid lockdowns, a few of us in our apartment complex formed a committee to deal with any emergency that might arise. This reassured the residents, especially the sick and elderly ones, that there was a mechanism and a system that would offer them help, should an emergency strike.

Be passionate. We must not mix happiness with success. In leadership guru Simon Sinek's words, 'Working hard for something we don't care about is called stress. Working hard for something we love unconditionally is called passion.' Passion is a precondition for excellence. Excellence is defined as an outstanding level of achievement in any field.

A person with passion will consistently overcome all obstacles, challenging themselves beyond what they know or can do well. The level of excellence is never static, not is the ability of passionate people to continuously improve and innovate in their fields of specialisation (as you'd have seen in the case of Jayashree's efforts to make miniatures over the years). The solution they arrive at, the paths they define, are almost always outside the box while being within the framework of reference.

On being passionate

Link 6: https://youtu.be/zOwMPPLeYJw
Duration: 01:39 Mts.

> On being Passionate: Philip McKernan wrote the book 'Rich on Paper - Poor on Life'. What he meant was, let us not mix happiness with success. Success does not lead to happiness. In fact, happiness leads to success. If we love what we are doing then we will definitely be successful and if we have to love what we are doing, we need to be passionate about it, even if we are able to pursue our passion on personal front, we will be successful on professional front. Lucky are those souls who are able to pursue their passion professionally, because passion helps one to unleash their genius. Here is a proof; get closer to many of those who have reached the fag end of their life and ask them for their regrets, invariably the inability to follow the passion will be one of them. So for us to be having a long, fulfilling and happy career, we should be able to identify our passion and follow it. The earlier we follow it, the better.

Their daily behaviour is reflected in the deep belief rooted in faith. Faith is a short word, but it has a deep implication. However, today, the problem is that people doubt their faith. Those with faith are of the belief that every next level of life will demand a better and different view. And hence, we need to be bolder. Passionate people don't fear changes. They embrace life as it comes.

Research shows that, towards the end of their lives, several people regret not having followed their passions when they could have.

Principles of success

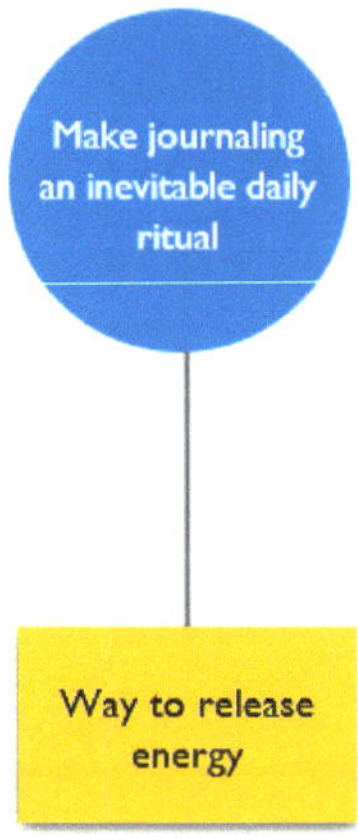

Always be positive

Journal every day. Journalling helps us record our daily experiences and thoughts, especially the ones that are out of the normal lot — experiences that are strange, that come to strike us and psyche us. It is always good to record these things and later, reflect on them to see what they taught us, what they shifted within us and what we could have done differently to handle them better.

Our subconscious records whatever we experience. Journalling helps bring these impressions up to our conscious mind. And when we encounter a similar situation or problem or experience again, our mind will find a way to address it better. In short, journalling helps us process problems and situations.

The benefits of journalling daily

Link 7: https://youtu.be/pZSgr5c1vyk
Duration: 02:36 Mts.

> The benefits of Journaling daily. All of us wants to succeed in life and a day is nothing but life lived in miniature form. We start the day expecting for a set of successful factors and then end the day with an experience.Things may not proceed as expected 'That is Life'. How do we enjoy this aspect, day in and day out? Well, things do happen in life for a reason. If we are able to understand it, we can keep moving forward, else, if we know that there is a parking lot in the form of Journal which we need to maintain at the end of every day religiously, we can always use it to reflect upon it later. Life is nothing but a set of natural and spectacular changes. If we are able to understand the changes and keep moving on it's great, else, if we know that there is a parking lot in the form of Journal, which can be referred to later. We can avoid the sorrows resulting from resisting the changes and keep moving on. We need to ensure that we don't allow the spectacular changes to be an obstacle in our path. If we can address the reasons for the changes reflected in the Journal at the end of every day, we can keep using the day for our plans for success. Otherwise, the problems reflected in the Journal, if not addressed on a regular basis, can become excuses. Success and excuses does not converse with each other. Later these problems can become excuses and come in the way of success. So, let us maintain the habit of Journaling our problems reason it out and allow the day to plan for success with full energy.

There's no particular method to journal. You just need to recollect your day from the start to the end. If you feel that there's something worth recording, you must record it in your daily journal.

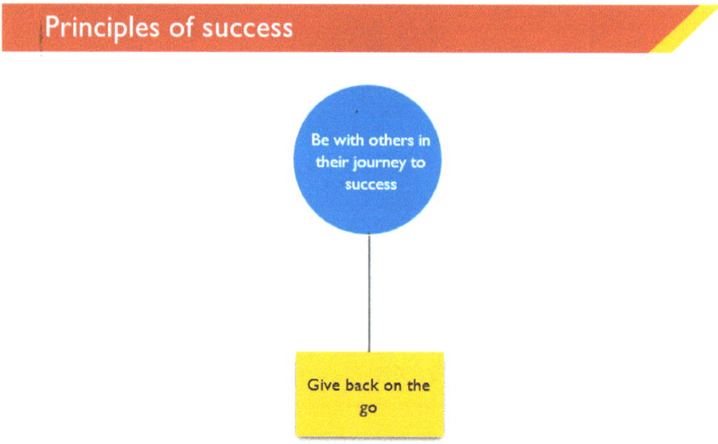

Always be positive

Everything negative in life can be shaped in a positive way. For instance, if we come across a colleague, subordinate or anyone else who is having a rough time and we find that they are not in great shape, we must take the initiative to reach out to them. Just a genuine word of reassurance that we are with them in their tough moments will help them. And then, it is better to stay calm, let them ride out the difficult moment and resume the conversation later, when they are feeling a little better. Otherwise, it might lead to a misunderstanding and strain the relationship.

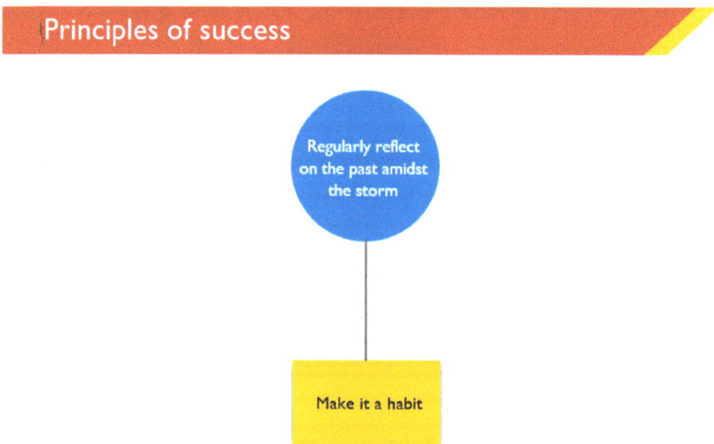

Always be positive

Our location is not a reason for us to not do well. If we have the right focus and the growth mindset, we will do well in any situation anywhere. This is what I experienced while working in Bombay, Hong Kong, Jakarta and then again in Bombay. And, when I was working in Jakarta, I was sent to several places such as Milan, the Philippines, Vietnam, China, Malaysia, Moscow and South Africa. These assignments used to last between a few days and a month. In each of these places, I faced a different ecosystem. I came across people who were of different cultures, background and moods. Some of them tended to be racist too!

However, I used to always find a way to get the necessary information, deal with the people and solve the problems I had been sent to solve. I was disciplined enough to ensure that I walked the talk and got things done. This mindset and ability have directly led to my career growth over the years.

Black Swan events like Covid-19 come once in a century. When they hit the world, there is bound to be all-round uncertainty. But these also offer great opportunities to experiment and introspect on what we are doing, as individuals and organisations, and change our course, if necessary.

This is what I did. I reviewed the journals I'd been writing over the past several years. This gave me an opportunity to introspect on my achievements, pitfalls and shortcomings and see what to improve.

Among other things, this helped me reflect on the business portfolio of Crown Worldwide-India and see if we should do anything differently. We brought in a few changes, from a customer-centric point of view, such as persuading our clients to digitise their paper records, and encouraged our team to develop more digital services to cater to our customers' hybrid mode of working.

Since most of the people were working from home, we allowed them access to the cloud system to test our new services from April 2020 to July 2020. This way, they got a feel of what was in store for them.

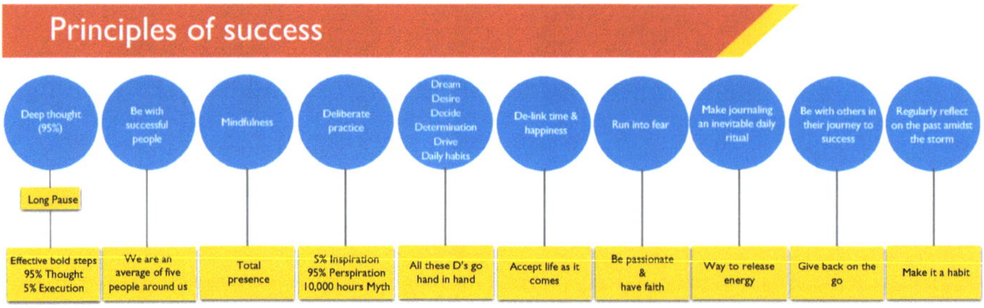

Always be positive

Key takeaways

Work hard in silence. Let your success be your noise.

Mindfulness and deliberate practice will enhance the quality and impact of our work.

Journalling every day is a great way to reflect on our thoughts and experiences and learning from them.

If you want something you have never had before, you must be willing to do something you have never done before. – Pastor Bill Purvis

Please provide your views, comments, feedback and share what parts of this chapter resonates with you here

Link: https://srinivas.powervisionelectrical.co.in/chapter-8-the-principles-of-sucess/

Chapter 9

Aspirations Need not Have Bounds

Your playing small does not serve the world.

– Marianne Williamson'

I love to set myself 'impossible' targets. And achieve them. I believe that the so-called impossible things can indeed happen. And this is borne out by several incidents in my life and in the lives of many others I know. At the heart of making the impossible happen is to believe in yourself even when no one else believes in you.

As I've said before, when I was transferred to Bombay from the Hong Kong office of Crown Worldwide, the India operations of Crown were in a bad state. In my new role, I was in charge of their India operations; the buck stopped with me. The world had just then experienced a financial collapse due to the Lehman Brothers debacle (this company went broke, and the entire sub-prime mortgage mess in the USA got exposed, sinking almost the whole world into a financial hole).

I found that almost everything that could go wrong was going wrong with Crown in India. We were losing customers and members of our team (very good members). And we were not able to honour even long-pending payment commitments to suppliers. God knows why. The morale was low all around. Almost all the branches of Crown in India were bent low due to service issues, defaults and what not.

Taking charge at such a time, I was shocked! My boss was based in Singapore. Most of his operations were doing quite well; India was the only underperformer. A dark horse.

I knew we had to do something out of the box to find a way out of the rubble.

So I set myself the seemingly-impossible target of becoming No. 1 in our line of business in India in 5 to 7 years. When I told my boss this, he laughed heartily, saying, 'You are finding it difficult to even stay afloat, and yet, you're talking about flying!' But I told him, and more importantly told *myself*, that unless we set the bar very high, unless we were *outrageously* ambitious, we were not going to find a way out of the hole.

My boss and team agreed. With their support, we did a whole host of things to clean up the operations. And we did manage to achieve my target in the stated time!

We could not have done this without the support of our team. They had to rally around the target I had set, make it their collective target and go after it. This phase taught me yet again that talent alone is not enough. You can have a great set of people, but you have to support them with the right infrastructure, the necessary motivation and the necessary tools. You have to give them direction and create the right culture at work. Only then can you get the best out of them. As we grow in our careers, the real test of our mettle is how we rally the people around us to give their best.

You need to be able to create a great team of people and ensure that all their reasonable needs are met. And create a fully functioning ecosystem that will support them.

When you're with a group of people who are moody and negative and are trying to put pressure on you without giving you adequate tools and other support, you can't do your best. You're never going to be able to think in the right way or focus on getting your inner strength. I saw this happen for several months in Crown when I started helming their India operations. It required some fresh, unconventional thinking to motivate our people and get them to dramatically improve their performance.

I see a lot of people not giving their best but being satisfied with their sub-optimal effort. Sub-optimal effort leads to sub-optimal results. Ask yourself what's stopping you from giving your best.

Do what others won't do.

Right from my youth, I've been doing what others have not done. I've often gone against the grain. As I have said before, when most people were moving from India to the Middle East for better jobs, I went to the Far East. And, when I had a good job in Hong Kong, I took a 'career-breaking step' by resigning from it when my three-year commitment was over. Further, while someone else would have found a better job in Hong Kong itself, I accepted an opportunity to work in Indonesia, which was far less economically developed than Hong Kong. But all this worked out very well for me!

You ought to set a direction for yourself and embrace the growth mindset. Be willing to slog it out to come up with something you can be proud of, when you look back later in life. When you introspect or when you face further challenges in your career, these are the things that will give you confidence.

I remember another time when I went against the grain. While most other companies were intent on scouting for talent in the market all the time (especially from our industry, which was anyway not having much talent), we at Crown-India created a crucible of talent *within* our company. We saw this as our perpetual in-house talent feed. We hired some promising candidates who had a few years of experience, got our training team to create a university of sorts within the company and moulded these people in our system and culture. This way, we created the right capabilities far more easily and at a much lower cost to the company. And the people we groomed internally got clear growth paths for their careers. Also, we didn't have to depend on knee-jerk reactions whenever someone quit our company and a post fell vacant.

I have found it vital to upskill myself from time to time. This has prepared me for not just bigger and better roles but also for sticky situations — when things go wrong. Keep adding skills to your skillset. And pushing the boundaries of what you think you can achieve.

One of the ways to upskill yourself is to take up courses. You could attend them on weekends and other holidays, and in your spare time in the evening. Also — and I have chosen this way — you can become a student of life. You can learn from every person and situation, constantly observe new developments in the market, learn new ways of doing things and never be satisfied with your achievements.

This becomes a culture of continuously improving yourself. When you do this — when you commit yourself to improving continuously — you will see your ecosystem also beginning to improve with you. People around you will try to emulate you. And that's how you inspire others and lift them along with yourself. You lift them when you're growing in your career, so all of you grow together as individuals and as a team.

If you have a history of doing things the right way, your effort, blessings and beliefs can go hand in hand. You can achieve more than what you think is possible. I call this sweat equity: what you earn by pouring enormous effort into what you want to achieve.

Just remember that, despite your imperfections, you are perfect in your own way. Many things cannot be perfect without you. So understand what you are good at and build upon that.

According to Irish psychologist Dr Philip McKernan, success is manufactured in the mind, while happiness is developed in the soul. So tune into your soulfulness. Let me explain. Whenever you're trying to fix a set of complicated problems, you can't expect to succeed overnight. You need to put your soul into finding a solution. And finding the solution to a complex issue takes time. While you can take a series of steps and start moving in the right direction, you will have to wait for the ultimate solution to crystallise. In this context, you must celebrate your small and big wins along the way. And you should make the other stakeholders also wait for the full and final outcome, though they may not have the patience for this. You will have to put your smarts to work here. A strong will and a deep belief in yourself will help you succeed ultimately, carrying the people in your ecosystem along with you.

The other thing to note is expectation versus acceptance. We all want the happiness chemical called 'peace of mind'. We realise that often, things do not go the way we want. Which is why I said earlier too that expectations can lead us to tears whereas acceptance can bring us cheers. According to Dr McKernan, seeking riches at the expense of our wellbeing exerts immense pressure on the spirit of the person who tries it.

Let me explain this concept of expectation versus acceptance with the example of my journey to the holy shrine of Lord Ayyappa in Sabarimala in Kerala. Every time we (I travel with a group of people) travel to this hilltop temple, we encounter a different set of challenges. The path is lined with stones or thorns, there are hundreds of leeches in the forested path, sometimes it rains heavily, sometimes the forest officials close the forest path midway, forcing us to take a detour … I could go on about the difficulties.

We deal with these difficulties by gearing our minds up in advance. The idea of embarking upon a pilgrimage is to take a break from our normal routine and find some piece of mind. It is a chance for us to introspect on our past, present and future. So we are in a calm, focused, determined state of mind, expecting that the journey will bring its share of difficulties. This, I think, is a pre-condition for peace of mind.

In general, I believe we should accept things as they are and try to overcome challenges with equanimity. And while doing this, it is not unreasonable to expect an outcome. But it is unreasonable to expect an outcome in a short period of time.

We should not lose our temper just because things don't turn out the way we want them to. At such junctures, we must stay the course and be patient. And sooner or later, we *will* accomplish our deep desire.

Life is best for those who enjoy it, difficult for those who analyse it too much and worst for those who criticise it. So I suggest you focus on your strengths, not on your so-called weaknesses or limitations. Focus on your character, not on your reputation. Focus on your blessings, not on your misfortunes.

Most of the problems that arise for anyone stem from their beliefs. If you fail at something for a long time, you may become the victim of certain limiting beliefs. Most of us seem to know all about limiting beliefs and fears. Some of us even talk about them. But merely knowing this does not change our life.

A belief is an idea that is held to be true. Beliefs are key components of our desire to grow and succeed. Beliefs shape and create the surface structures of our thoughts and actions. Our beliefs determine how events are given meaning, and are the essence of our motivation. So, limiting beliefs can keep you in a negative state of mind and hinder your growth. They can keep you from encountering new opportunities.

The other thing is our doubts. Our doubts keep us from making any choice that involves change. Some of our important choices have a time frame. If we delay a decision, the opportunity may be lost forever. So, if you want to do something, just do it, always believing that it is for the best. Just because we encountered failure in the past it doesn't mean that we have lost our abilities forever and will fail in future too.

In this context, it is important to understand the law of wasted effort. Do you know that lions succeed in only a quarter of their hunting attempts? Which means they fail in 75% of their attempts and succeed only in 25% of them! It's the same story with most other predators too. Despite this small percentage of success, the animals don't despair. Because they are intuitively aware of the law of wasted effort. This understanding has been naturally wired into them.

Half of the eggs of fish get eaten; they never hatch. Half the baby bears die before puberty. Most of the world's rain falls into oceans; most of the seeds of the fruit are eaten by birds. Scientists have found that animals, trees and other elements of nature are more receptive to the law of wasted effort. This is a universal law.

It is only we humans who don't get it. We think that if we do something once, we must immediately succeed. And if we fail in the one or two attempts we make, we think it is the end of the world and whine. Worse, we give up the pursuit altogether! But the truth is that we fail only when we don't try at all, or stop trying. Success is not to have a life free of pitfalls, losses and rejections. It is to walk past our mistakes and go beyond rejections and failure at every stage.

So, if you don't succeed in your attempts, remember the law of wasted effort and rewire your belief system to help you continue all over again.

This is the key to success. Also, don't try to preempt a solution before studying the problem properly; casually diagnosing the causes and giving up after a half-hearted attempt or two is also a common problem. It will likely lead you to failure.

Of course, the experience of having dealt with challenges gives us great confidence. But it does not guarantee success. Every situation must be handled on its merit — based on the intensity and complexity of the issue at hand. We have to deal with the inevitable obstacles on our journey to success. And for this, we need to have the right mindset. This is what I have tried to have all along, in every aspect of my life, especially in my career.

Key takeaways

Victory is much more meaningful when it comes not just from the effort of one person but from the joint achievements of many. – American businessman Howard Schultz

Set 'impossible' targets.

Give your best. Sub-optimal efforts lead to sub-optimal results.

Understand what you are good at and build on it.

Your aspirations for yourself can be sky-high.

Try to overcome challenges with equanimity.

Please provide your views, comments, feedback and share what parts of this chapter resonates with you here

Link: https://srinivas.powervisionelectrical.co.in/chapter-9-aspirations-need-not-have-bounds/

Chapter 10

The Hidden Hand in my Success

If I have grown, crossed milestones and won laurels in my professional life, it is, to a large extent, because of one person. If I have been able to straddle the professional arenas in cricket and corporate life, it is, to a large measure, because of that same person. If I have been able to lead a comfortable life for the past 25 years and pay enough attention to my fitness and other priorities, it is again, to a great degree, because of that same person.

Jayashree, my wife.

Of course, my parents, paternal grandmother and maternal grandfather laid the foundation for my growth. But from the time I got married to Jayashree, she has been the prime mover behind my growth and success.

A wonderful life partner is a must for a person to be successful. They can spur the person into becoming better, doing their best and reaching great heights. By taking care of several important aspects of the person's life, their partner clears the way for their growth, happiness and success.

Jayashree and I got married in the conventional way (remember, it was the late 1990s, in India). I belong to an era where we still trusted the judgment of our parents and believed in matching horoscopes. After serving in a company in Hong Kong for three years, I'd left the job and gone to London for a week, just to go berserk. And, after a week of fun and frolic there, I spent about three weeks in Bombay before heading back to Hong Kong.

When I was in Bombay, my dad arranged for me to meet a few girls — prospective alliances, as we called them. Dad's way of finding an alliance for me was to see if a girl's horoscope matched mine. If it did, we'd graduate to the next level and meet other each. This way, I ended up meeting a few girls. Jayashree was one of them.

Being a religious person, I went to the Mahalaxmi temple along the bay area in Bombay and prayed that whatever decision I took regarding my marriage be the right one. And then I went to meet Jayashree, who was then working with Vijaya Bank. I met her in a restaurant near her office in South Bombay.

I was a reasonably open-minded person. I didn't have any great expectations from the girl I would eventually marry. Except, I was adamant that she should not want to make a career after marriage. I know, I know, this thought is so outdated. But that's how I was back then. I'd made up my mind at a very young age that I would climb the ladder of professional success. And I thought that having a working spouse would lay a lot of barriers in my path. So, though it was the wrong way to think, I put this up as one of the conditions for marriage.

But Jayashree immediately accepted it! She asked me just one thing: whether I drank or smoked. I said I didn't do either. That's all she wanted, apparently. And we both agreed to take the matter forward.

But then, two days later, my parents said that we couldn't marry because, for whatever reason, among the ten parameters that were meant to be mapped and matched on our horoscopes, only about six were matching. At least eight of those parameters had to match for a 'satisfactory marriage', they said.

I didn't know anything about these things. So I left the matter there and went off to the holy town of Tirupati. There, I had my head tonsured (that was a thing among pilgrims to Tirupati; it still is), prayed at the temple and, two days before I was to leave for Hong Kong, returned to Bombay.

My dad said, 'There is news for you.'

I asked him, 'What?'

He replied, 'I went back to the astrologer and pressed him to look at your and Jayashree's horoscopes with a sharper eye. And he has pronounced that the two of them do match!' It was a pleasant surprise for me. I think I let out an inward sigh of relief.

The next day, tonsured head and all, I met Jayashree and her family. About five of my family members came along. Jayashree's family members were confused for a moment, wondering who the would-be groom was. I could see their eyes quickly roaming over our group, trying to find the person whose photo they had seen earlier. It was when Jayashree pointed me out that they all realised that I, the bald guy who had given away all his hair to the Lord in Tirupati, was the groom. There was a bit of laughter all around. Jayashree's parents were sceptical about me initially, but then, decided that everything was alright and we could go ahead with the marriage.

As it happened, I got the job offer from Crown Worldwide-Indonesia — a particularly good offer — at around the same time. I told myself, 'It's only after I agreed to marry this girl that I got this opportunity. So she is the right person for me.'

That was more than 25 years ago.

So much has happened since then; so much has changed for the better since then. But one thing hasn't changed: Jayashree continues to be the pillar of my life. And indeed, of our whole family. She has been the harbinger of several good things in my life — better jobs, my playing in the Jakarta provincial cricket team and the Indonesia national cricket team, domestic bliss, and so many other things. I can't voice my gratitude enough.

All these years, she has pretty much taken care of our household singlehandedly, while I have been travelling, handling the pressures at work, playing professional cricket and building my career. I could be away at work for a week, and she would ensure that everything was taken care of. She's the one to be credited for the upbringing and happy childhood of our children and for the fact that they have grown up into fine people today.

She has some great qualities: a keen sixth sense, the ability to think ahead of a situation, the tact to handle any situation. And of course, she has been a great homemaker and artist. She draws and knits very well and makes those wonderful miniatures that I spoke of earlier. Of the two of us, she's the more creatively endowed. She's an out-of-the-box thinker. She's great at building relationships too. And she always knows how to maintain a balance in anything, including in life itself.

A postgraduate in Commerce, she has learned cost accountancy and has a degree in banking. She worked in a public sector bank in India for 5 or 6 years before we got married. All this sharpened her professional abilities.

But she willingly forsook these and her ambition for my sake — so that *I* could grow professionally and chase my dreams. All along, she's cheered me, given me superb opinions and advice to tackle various knotty situations, told me where I was going off-kilter and generally kept me on track.

It is impossible to quantify the benefits I have enjoyed in these 25 years because of her presence in my life.

I especially recall our stint in Indonesia — probably because it was a slightly more complicated and demanding phase of our life. Our children were very little, so they needed constant care and attention. And then, I used to throw these parties for our clients and the Indian diaspora — for instance, on Diwali eve. Jayashree used to organise these parties so well! She'd come up with novel games and prizes and find a way to keep the kids engaged.

And when it was time for our crucial move back to India in 2010 to take care of our aging parents, she was totally in step with me. Moving from our 6-bedroom mansion in Jakarta, she strapped herself down and adjusted to life in a tiny apartment in a congested suburb of Bombay. Difficult, but she took it in her stride and kept doing what she did best, every day.

I was especially touched by how she took care of my father when he was sick. It was her presence and close attention that induced a turnaround in him: he went from bedridden to almost active! She attended to his every need while I was busy at work. During the same period one day, she had the foresight to rush my mother to the hospital, virtually carrying her, sensing that something was seriously wrong with her. It turned out that my mother had contracted swine flu from one of my relatives who visited us from overseas. Jayashree's quick action saved Mom's life.

Her benign presence in my life has changed my attitude and my perspective on life. For the better, of course. I berate myself for ignoring her suggestions in the early years of our marriage. But, as the years went by, I realised that she has a keen insight into situations, people, relationships and life itself. So I wisened up and started paying heed to whatever she said. I've learned a lot about understanding people from her.

She does lament occasionally that she had to give up her career and her passions for the sake of my career and our family. Every person wants to live their life *their* way, do the things they want to do. And they have every right to do so. It is weird that only one person in our marriage has grown professionally and that this growth has come at the cost of the other person's growth and sense of fulfillment. This is not healthy.

I wish I had realised this 25 years ago. Then I would have let her grow in her career; we could have grown together. I regret that I did not support her in household affairs and in her career. This regret will remain with me for life. But now, I am trying to make amends for it, to whatever extent I can. In the last five years or so, after our kids finished their schooling, Jayashree has taken up some of her old hobbies.

In 2017, she started teaching children maths. She joined this well-known institute called Cuemath as a maths teacher. For her stellar work, she won the Hall of Fame award at this institute. Further, Cuemath requested her to evaluate new teachers who joined the institute. And in this capacity, she won the Golden Globe Award for her superb work. As a result, she was invited to join a select band of teachers under an initiative called Cuemath Plus. These teachers teach kids offline and online.

When Covid-19 struck, Jayashree started teaching maths to children across the world. She has helped several children shed their fear of and dislike for maths and learn it with joy. She is a shining example of the maxim 'form is temporary, but class is permanent'. I am overjoyed that after sacrificing her dreams for so many years for the sake of her family, she is finally back on the professional track. And doing extremely well.

But then, her health has taken a beating. We are trying our best to get it to improve. I am confident that she will be fully well soon.

It's been 25 years since we got married, and it's been a fantastic journey for us. It's difficult to imagine a life without Jayashree.

Key takeaways

Please ensure that you and your partner grow together, personally and professionally.

Aim for healthy, balanced growth as a couple. Support your partner in every way and be there for them in every important situation.

Help them achieve their dreams, just as you'd want them to help you achieve yours.

Please provide your views, comments, feedback and share what parts of this chapter resonates with you here

Link: https://srinivas.powervisionelectrical.co.in/chapter-10-the-hidden-hand-in-my-success/

Looking Ahead

I am encouraged by the life I've led so far. I have learned a lot, and it has been fulfilling. I am happy I am in a position to pass on my learnings and joys to the next generation. I think the best way to live life is to look beyond oneself and beyond one's daily routine. Learning new things and continuously upskilling oneself, keeping oneself fit, making progress in every aspect of life — not just financially but also spiritually and in many other ways — and caring for one's family are what help us thrive and succeed.

I am grateful for whatever life has given me. I think of each day as an adventure, akin to ziplining, white water rafting and trekking: brimming with thrill, joy, curiosity and wonder at the vistas it brings. I hope to keep this spirit alive forever.

Please provide your feedback in www.srinivassk.com

Chapter Summary: Poke the Bear Within!

PREFACE

Unveiling Greatness: A Path Beyond Material Riches / Unveiling the Path to Lasting Fulfilment

Embark on a captivating voyage through the inspiring life journey of an accomplished individual who has risen from humble beginnings to become an influential member of the Executive Leadership Team at Crown Worldwide Group. This remarkable individual's story takes us on a transformative path filled with valuable life lessons, principles, and values that have shaped his success. Through the highs and lows, he has discovered the true meaning of richness – beyond material wealth. In this book, you will explore the essence of gratitude, hope, and happiness, as well as the importance of embracing life's challenges as the finest teacher. Get ready to unlock the secrets to achieving greatness and leading a fulfilling, successful life through personal anecdotes and insightful experiences. Whether you seek professional success or personal growth, this book offers practical wisdom for readers from all walks of life.

Chapter 1 - Always Expect More from Yourself Than from Others / The Pursuit of Excellence: Setting Self as the Standard

Dive into an entrancing narrative that delves into complexities of life's diverse roles and the expectations that accompany them. This chapter offers valuable insights on finding inspiration by setting higher standards for oneself rather than being burdened by external expectations. Discover the power of introspection, incremental improvement, and ruthless discipline to achieve personal growth and success. The author's journey, from pursuing a passion for cricket to excelling in the corporate world, showcases the importance of focus and determination in achieving one's dreams. Prepare to be inspired and motivated to embrace self-improvement and carve a fulfilling path to success in various aspects of life.

Chapter 2 - From Humble Beginnings to Corporate Success: Embracing Life's Lessons / From Modesty to Corporate Eminence: Embracing Life's Lessons

Venture into a riveting chronicle that traverses the life of the author who began from humble beginnings but soared to unprecedented heights within the corporate domain. This tale illuminates the pivotal role played by his kin, comrades, and the personal experiences that shaped the trajectory of his success. The story emphasizes the different experiences of his life that have helped shape a path to success. It showcases the influence of his grandparents and parents in instilling valuable life lessons, hard work, and determination. Through a series of significant decisions, the author navigates challenges, seizes opportunities, and breaks away from the norm. With a contrarian approach, the protagonist sets out to work abroad, eventually achieving recognition and accolades in the corporate realm. The tale is a testament to the power of resilience, self-belief, and the impact of life's invaluable teachings.

Chapter 3 - A Journey of Character and Resilience / Fusing Cricket's Crucible with Life's Crucibles

Engage with an evocative chronicle celebrating the transformative power of sports, particularly cricket, in the protagonist's life. Here, we unveil the profound role of passion in shaping lessons of teamwork, grit, and personal growth. From childhood memories to navigating the challenges of academic and professional pursuits, the author's experiences on and off the cricket field have profoundly influenced his life's trajectory. Readers can expect to explore essential life lessons drawn from cricket, including the importance of leadership, building winning teams, and maintaining a positive attitude in various aspects of life. This section will resonate with anyone seeking inspiration and valuable takeaways from the world of sports and personal development.

Chapter 4 - Expedition of Lifelong Learning / Unveiling the Mind's Potential

This chapter ushers readers into a fascinating foray of self-discovery and personal evolution propelled by the potency of erudition. We embark on an enlightening expedition of self-discovery. Here, we experience the power of learning. The discourse probes the boundlessness of our learning capacity, unveiling that judicious guidance is the sole prerequisite to unshackling it. The writer shares personal anecdotes, drawing lessons from his experiences and mentors, highlighting the significance of applied learning and different learning styles. This chapter delves into the impact of technology on learning, the importance of active listening, and the drawbacks of digital overreliance. Additionally, we will see the emphasis on the value of failure as a steppingstone to success and the role of exercise in enhancing brain performance. With practical insights and valuable takeaways, this presentation aims to empower readers to embrace learning as their superpower to thrive in the ever-changing world.

Chapter 5 - Thriving Beyond Boundaries / Conquering New Horizons

Here, we are on a trajectory of personal maturation and professional advancement that will take you on a journey of personal growth and professional development. It narrates the experiences of an individual who stepped out of his comfort zone to pursue career opportunities abroad. Here, we will be able to see that through vivid anecdotes, the chapter highlights the challenges of adapting to a new country, including cultural shocks, financial struggles, and the importance of self-reliance. You will gain insights into the Asian financial crisis and how it presented a unique business opportunity for the writer. It emphasizes the value of gaining experience in the field and the pivotal role of adaptability in navigating life's changes. Here, you'll find valuable life lessons, such as the significance of continuous learning, the role of resilience in facing adversity, and the importance of cherishing the connections we make along life's journey. Thus, peer into a life sewn by global odysseys and unyielding growth, enriched with essential life wisdom and the significance of relationships.

Chapter 6 - Cultivating The Victorious Mindset / Cultivating Mastery

Plunge into the enthralling realm of mindset and its transformative sway on growth. The importance of developing the right mindset and its impact on personal and professional growth is seen and understood here. The author shares his personal experiences and insights on cultivating a growth mindset, problem-solving, saying 'no' when required, gratitude, and the power of positive thinking. The chapter also emphasizes the significance of focusing on priorities, staying humble, and being generous. The role of health and meditation in shaping a successful mindset is explored, along with the significance of continuous learning and adaptability. Through real-life anecdotes and lessons, the author encourages readers to embrace change, handle challenges creatively, and unlock their full potential for a fulfilling life and career.

Chapter 7 - Nurturing Bonds for Growth / The Tapestry of Relationships

Embark on an insightful discourse dissecting the profound impact of relationships on personal and professional evolution. From the perspective of an experienced individual, readers will explore the transformative power of self-awareness and compassion in forging meaningful connections. Here, you'll find valuable principles for establishing and maintaining strong relationships with colleagues and people from diverse backgrounds. Through personal anecdotes and experiences, readers will gain practical tips for effective communication, conflict resolution, and the art of forgiveness. As readers, we will be inspired to embrace a mindset of gratitude, cherish the present, and count our blessings. It concludes with essential reminders to cherish and cultivate relationships while setting healthy boundaries and maintaining self-respect.

Chapter 8 - Navigating Success's Labyrinth / The Arc of Excellence

Navigate a kaleidoscope that unlocks diverse insights and pragmatic sagacity on personal evolution, creativity, mindfulness, purposeful practice, passion, faith, and conquering challenges. It emphasizes the importance of deep thought and long pauses in decision-making, taking bold steps, and consulting experienced mentors to avoid or mitigate risks. It showcases the significance of imagination and creativity in problem-solving and achieving success. Furthermore, it delves into deliberate practice and dispels myths around the 10,000-hour rule. It highlights the role of desire, determination, and daily habits in pursuing dreams and achieving excellence. The importance of forging connections, embracing change, and maintaining a growth mindset is also discussed. The author shares personal experiences to illustrate the power of a positive mindset, resilience, and adaptability, particularly during challenging times like the Covid-19 pandemic. Overall, readers can expect to gain valuable insights and practical strategies for personal and professional growth, success, and self-improvement.

Chapter 9 - Defying the Odds for Achievement / Conquering the Unconquerable

Partake in an inspiring chapter documenting a voyage of transcending seemingly insurmountable odds to achieve extraordinary success. The saga revolves around the personal journey of overcoming seemingly impossible challenges and achieving remarkable success. The story revolves around the author's role in reviving the struggling India operations of Crown Worldwide during a global financial crisis. Setting ambitious goals and believing in oneself despite doubts from others proved to be the driving force behind his achievements. The protagonist emphasizes the importance of building a strong team, providing the right support and culture, and constantly upskilling oneself to overcome obstacles. He shares valuable lessons on resilience, perseverance, and the significance of accepting challenges with equanimity. The audience will gain insights into the power of mindset, the impact of beliefs and doubts, and how the law of wasted effort can lead to greater success. This inspires individuals to set high targets, embrace growth, and focus on their strengths to achieve extraordinary results in their personal and professional lives.

Chapter 10 - Love's Role in Growth and Triumph / A Beacon of Growth and Triumph

In this heartfelt account, we embark on a remarkable journey of personal and professional growth, where the author attributes much of his success and achievements to one person - his wife, Jayashree. This touching story spans over 25 years of their married life, showcasing how a supportive and caring life partner can become the driving force behind one's success. Set in the late 1990s in India, we witness how destiny and astrology played a role in bringing them together. With a glimpse into their early struggles and joys, we learn how Jayashree's selflessness and unwavering support paved the way for her husband's career while putting aside her own dreams. However, the narrative doesn't end there, as we witness Jayashree's resurgence in her professional life through her dedication to teaching maths to children worldwide. This chapter encapsulates love's essence, sacrifice's nobility, and growth's allure, leaving readers invigorated and contemplating the role of a supportive confidant in achieving both personal and vocational milestones.

Appendix: My videos on YouTube

For your benefits today and for the foreseeable future.

Morning Mantra from Srini		
Sr No	**Description**	**Link to the video**
1	On being connected with charismatic people	https://youtu.be/H4tdUp-SIt8
2	On learning, living, loving and growing	https://youtu.be/1ziJDTekqmY
3	A viewpoint on what life is all about	https://youtu.be/_9NcDNqsQps
4	Learning new things regularly	https://youtu.be/l8yrHVA48nM

Morning Mantra from Srini		
Sr No	**Description**	**Link to the video**
5	Zygomaticus - on smiling	https://youtu.be/6LljFDEL1T8
6	On tough times	https://youtu.be/CzWCTRyMb3w
7	On getting a kick in the back	https://youtu.be/F4Mu-lTVQo4
8	On relationships	https://youtu.be/MrZeCQPJquw
9	On being rich	https://youtu.be/3eplXOjon1Y
10	On letting someone go	https://youtu.be/8irFZajGZP4

Morning Mantra from Srini		
Sr No	**Description**	**Link to the video**
11	On invoking positivity	https://youtu.be/c0lY0NMUeNY
12	Another tool to spur positivity in life	https://youtu.be/Lvi6TPgIHy8
13	On thoughts	https://youtu.be/IzY5KsfwXvU
14	On feelings and expectations	https://youtu.be/XYmLrJY2M0g
15	On will power	https://youtu.be/opSv5N3lsKQ
16	On applying knowledge and ideas	https://youtu.be/QwIysHykx6Y

Morning Mantra from Srini		
Sr No	**Description**	**Link to the video**
17	On saying yes and no	https://youtu.be/TesqlJutfxE
18	On developing relationships	https://youtu.be/fxO1d6buP8c
19	On handling worries	https://youtu.be/rNE7tmIU-Ew
20	On exercising leadership	https://youtu.be/xxzBtpaNx2U
21	On being humble	https://youtu.be/Dwl4uWJbEMA
22	On respecting and managing time	https://youtu.be/ieObiLHy4-o

Morning Mantra from Srini		
Sr No	**Description**	**Link to the video**
23	On making things easy like crazy	https://youtu.be/G2PfQEe7uFI
24	The S-square of solutions for life	https://youtu.be/wFafo-9hR6E
25	The secret of greatness	https://youtu.be/TrRKPT4MUQs
26	The benefit of spending time alone	https://youtu.be/IM3Z8M-ZCV8
27	On enriching oneself	https://youtu.be/3hOPd5rVMFY
28	On guarding against addiction	https://youtu.be/uNGn91x59EM

Morning Mantra from Srini		
Sr No	**Description**	**Link to the video**
29	The power of right connections	https://youtu.be/qc0gpyHy46I
30	The futile search for a beautiful tomorrow	https://youtu.be/zk5jECZwojY
31	Those little things in life	https://youtu.be/sBwqljgt5Xs
32	The 5 Cs to craft a growing life	https://youtu.be/ji3-2dmyYlA
33	On using friendship and love as healers	https://youtu.be/zci-38iYD_o
34	Invoking the power of the mind	https://youtu.be/Rs4s3GblcNE

Morning Mantra from Srini		
Sr No	**Description**	**Link to the video**
35	Chasing success v/s happiness	https://youtu.be/QFY9rfC4ZHs
36	The key to the door of personal excellence	https://youtu.be/CieNuZaZKMc
37	A measure of a person's worth	https://youtu.be/M9AAptkBRz8
38	View problems as situations	https://youtu.be/R_4cOlsg_1k
39	The fallacy of multi-tasking	https://youtu.be/F8RprRWwC7w
40	Making the most of an uncertain life	https://youtu.be/X5FymyNSUEQ

Morning Mantra from Srini		
Sr No	**Description**	**Link to the video**
41	Merits of spending time alone	https://youtu.be/iu2vRjxtlfg
42	The secrets of growth - Series 1 of 5 (from 10 years of my experience)	https://youtu.be/DMyyWgpwO6w
43	The secrets of growth - Series 2 of 5 (my experience since 2010). For those who missed Series 1, please watch it to understand the connection between Series 1 and Series 2.	https://youtu.be/IA4_dpk6tnE
44	The secrets of growth - Series 3 of 5	https://youtu.be/_ge0PPWFTkQ
45	The secrets of growth - Series 4 of 5	https://youtu.be/mR70ya0DY1U
46	The search for growth - Series 5 of 5	https://youtu.be/JpVO8Eqa1GA

Morning Mantra from Srini		
Sr No	**Description**	**Link to the video**
47	The power of the '+' symbol in life	https://youtu.be/L8q28r8_3Dg
48	Clue to the relationship with zeroes - on maintaining relationships	https://youtu.be/QIwnIn-To-k
49	The social service conundrum - expectation vs acceptance	https://youtu.be/q7bUSZNHt3M
50	The edge for being successful - and the need to sustain it	https://youtu.be/zUGGsIGqErQ
51	How to be an achiever forever - solving the dilemma between prestige and honour	https://youtu.be/ShA5ysR5P5g
52	The benefits of journalling daily - journalling at the end of the day can release energy for planning future success	https://youtu.be/pZSgr5c1vyk

Morning Mantra from Srini		
Sr No	Description	Link to the video
53	On being passionate - 'Success is manufactured in mind, while happiness is developed in the soul.' - Irish psychologist Phil Mckernan	https://youtu.be/zOwMPPLeYJw
54	The myth of linking happiness with time	https://youtu.be/ZJXlbzt7MhQ
55	Traits of a growth mindset	https://www.youtube.com/watch?v=b2HInbYxL58
56	What is deliberate practice?	https://www.youtube.com/watch?v=h4JbjT09n8s
57	Navratri 2021 - Amarnath Yatra	https://youtu.be/cZTnGfU78Bo

www.ingramcontent.com/pod-product-compliance
Lightning Source LLC
LaVergne TN
LVHW051134210926
848482LV00006B/314

* 9 7 9 8 8 9 1 3 3 3 6 3 5 *